A Nancy Willard Reader

The Bread Loaf Series of Contemporary Writers

NANCY WILLARD

A Nancy Willard
READER

SELECTED

POETRY AND PROSE

Middlebury College Press
Published by University Press of New England
Hanover and London

MIDDLEBURY COLLEGE PRESS
Published by University Press of New England,
Hanover, NH 03755
© 1991 by Nancy Willard
All rights reserved
Acknowledgments appear on page 219
Printed in the United States of America   5   4   3   2   1

CIP data appear at the end of the book

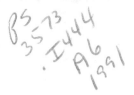

FOR ERIC AND JAMES

Contents

vii

Contents

A Bread Loaf Contemporary

A T   A   T I M E when the literary world is increasingly dominated by commercial formulas and concentrated financial power, there is a clear need to restore the simple pleasures of reading: the experience of opening a book by an author you know and being delighted by a completely new dimension of her or his art, the joy of seeing an author break free of any formula to reveal the power of the well-written word. The best writing, many authors affirm, comes as a gift; the best reading comes when the author passes that gift to the reader, a gift the author could imagine only by taking risks in a variety of genres including short stories, poetry, and essays.

As editors of The Bread Loaf Series of Contemporary Writers we subscribe to no single viewpoint. Our singular goal is to publish writing that moves the reader: by the beauty and lucidity of its language, by its underlying argument, by its force of vision. These values are celebrated each summer at the Writers' Conference on Bread Loaf Mountain in Vermont and in each of these books.

We offer you the Bread Loaf Contemporary Writers series and the treasures with which these authors have surprised us.

Robert Pack
Jay Parini

The Reader Inquires, the Author Answers

Dear Ms. Willard,

A friend of mine recently loaned me a copy of your novel, *Things Invisible to See*. I notice that you have the same name as the person who wrote *A Visit to William Blake's Inn: Poems for Innocent and Experienced Travelers*. Are you the same person? If so, why do you work in such different genres? Who is your audience?

Sincerely,

A.R.

A.R.

Dear A.R.,

Yes, the same person wrote the two books you mention, and yes, I am that person. If you happen to run across a collection of poems called *Water Walker* or another one called *Household Tales of Moon and Water*, I'll take responsibility for those, too. Also for a couple of collections of short stories.

To answer your question about working in different genres: each work chooses its own form, and I try to follow its lead—story, poem, novel, or essay. I hope the connections between them are clear. They all come from the same well, a metaphor I don't take lightly.

When I was growing up in Ann Arbor, Michigan, I heard plenty of stories about folks coming into the world and going out of it and maybe coming back once in a while to keep an eye on us, the living. Call them guardians, ancestors, spirits; they glistened before us in a web of words: their stories were the gifts they handed down to us.

Behind their gifts lay questions: *What will you give to those who come after? Who do you want to be?*

Why, the village storyteller, of course. The children sit in the front rows, the parents and the grandparents gather in the back. May my story or poem be as lucky as a lost traveler whose road finds him and leads him home. May it delight travelers, like a gift from the ancestors.

Nancy Willard

POEMS

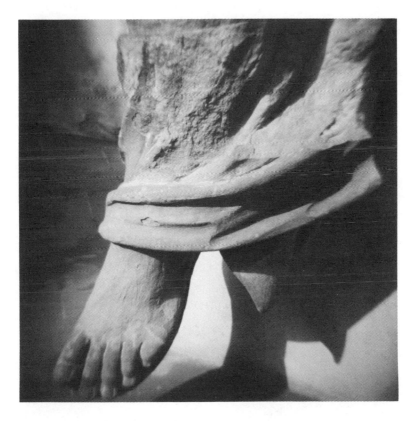

Questions My Son Asked Me,
Answers I Never Gave Him

1. Do gorillas have birthdays?
   Yes. Like the rainbow, they happen.
   Like the air, they are not observed.

2. Do butterflies make a noise?
   The wire in the butterfly's tongue
   hums gold.
   Some men hear butterflies
   even in winter.

3. Are they part of our family?
   They forgot us, who forgot how to fly.

4. Who tied my navel? Did God tie it?
   God made the thread: O man, live forever!
   Man made the knot: enough is enough.

5. If I drop my tooth in the telephone
   will it go through the wires and bite someone's ear?
   I have seen earlobes pierced by a tooth of steel.
   It loves what lasts.
   It does not love flesh.
   It leaves a ring of gold in the wound.

6. If I stand on my head
   will the sleep in my eye roll up into my head?
   Does the dream know its own father?
   Can bread go back to the field of its birth?

7. Can I eat a star?
   Yes, with the mouth of time
   that enjoys everything.

8. Could we Xerox the moon?
   This is the first commandment:

I am the moon, thy moon.
Thou shalt have no other moons before thee.

9. Who invented water?
   The hands of the air, that wanted to wash each other.

10. What happens at the end of numbers?
    I see three men running toward a field.
    At the edge of the tall grass, they turn into light.

11. Do the years ever run out?
    God said, I will break time's heart.
    Time ran down like an old phonograph.
    It lay flat as a carpet.
    At rest on its threads, I am learning to fly.

In Praise of Unwashed Feet

Because I can walk over hot coals,
because I can make doctors turn green
and shoe salesmen avert their eyes,
because I have added yet another use
to the hundred and one uses of Old Dutch Cleanser;
because they tell me the secrets of miners and small boys,
because they keep me in good standing and continual grace
in the ashes and dust of the last rites,
because they carry my great bulk without complaint,
because they don't smell;
because it's taken me years
to grow my own shoes, like the quaint signatures of truth,
because they are hard and gentle as lion's pads,
pard's paw, mule's hoof and cock's toes,
because they can't make poems or arguments
but speak in an aching tongue or not at all
and come home at night encrusted with stones,
calluses, grass, all that the head forgets
      and the foot knows.

When There Were Trees

I can remember when there were trees,
great tribes of spruces who deckled themselves in light,
beeches buckled in pewter, meeting like Quakers,
the golden birch, all cutwork satin,
courtesan of the mountains; the paper birch
trying all summer to take off its clothes
like the swaddlings of the newborn.

The hands of a sassafras blessed me.
I saw maples fanning the fire in their stars,
heard the coins of the aspens rattling like teeth,
saw cherry trees spraying fountains of light,
smelled the wine my heel pressed from ripe apples,
saw a thousand planets bobbing like bells
on the sleeve of the sycamore, chestnut, and lime.

The ancients knew that a tree is worthy of worship.
A few wise men from their tribes broke through the sky,
climbing past worlds to come and the rising moon
on the patient body of the tree of life,
and brought back the souls of the newly slain,
no bigger than apples, and dressed the tree
as one of themselves and danced.

Even the conquerors of this country
lifted their eyes and found the trees
more comely than gold: *Bright green trees,*
the whole land so green it is pleasure to look on it,
and the greatest wonder to see the diversity.
During that time, I walked among trees,
the most beautiful things I had ever seen.*

Watching the shadows of trees, I made peace with mine.
Their forked darkness gave motion to morning light.

**Adapted from the journals of Christopher Columbus, as rendered in William
Carlos Williams's* In the American Grain.

Every night the world fell to the shadows,
and every morning came home, the dogwood floating
its petals like moons on a river of air,
the oak kneeling in wood sorrel and fern,
the willow washing its hair in the stream.

And I saw how the logs from the mill floated
downstream, saw otters and turtles that rode them,
and though I heard the saws whine in the woods
I never thought men were stronger than trees.
I never thought those tribes would join
the buffalo and the whale, the leopard, the seal, the wolf,
and the folk of this country who knew how to sing them.

Nothing I ever saw washed off the sins of the world
so well as the first snow dropping on trees.
We shoveled the pond clear and skated under their branches,
our voices muffled in their huge silence.
The trees were always listening to something else.
They didn't hear the beetle with the hollow tooth
grubbing for riches, gnawing for empires, for gold.

Already the trees are a myth,
half gods, half giants in whom nobody believes.
But I am the oldest woman on earth,
and I can remember when there were trees.

How to Stuff a Pepper

Now, said the cook, I will teach you
how to stuff a pepper with rice.

Take your pepper green, and gently,
for peppers are shy. No matter which side
you approach, it's always the backside.
Perched on green buttocks, the pepper sleeps.
In its silk tights, it dreams
of somersaults and parsley,
of the days when the sexes were one.

Slash open the sleeve
as if you were cutting a paper lantern,
and enter a moon, spilled like a melon,
a fever of pearls,
a conversation of glaciers.
It is a temple built to the worship
of morning light.

I have sat under the great globe
of seeds on the roof of that chamber,
too dazzled to gather the taste I came for.
I have taken the pepper in hand,
smooth and blind, a runt in the rich
evolution of roses and ferns.
You say I have not yet taught you

to stuff a pepper?
Cooking takes time.

Next time we'll consider the rice.

Moss

A green sky underfoot:
the skin of moss
holds the footprints of
star-footed birds.

With moss-fingers, with
filigree they line
their nests in the
forks of the trees.

All around, the apples
are falling, the leaves
snap, the sun moves
away from the earth.

Only the moss stays,
decently covers the
roots of things, itself
rooted in silence:

rocks coming alive
underfoot, rain no
man heard fall. Moss,
stand up for us,

the small birds and
the great sun. You know
our trees and apples,
our parrots and women's eyes.

Keep us in your green
body, laid low
and still blossoming
under the snow.

Onionlight

Sacks crammed with light, layer on luminous layer,
an underworld calendar, the peeled pages faintly lined
but printed without month or measure
and pure as the damp kiss of a pearl,

as if the rings in an old tree should suddenly separate
and bracelet the axe; I have stooped among onions all morning,
hunting these flightless birds as they perched among roots.
I have yanked them out by the tail

and dropped them into my bag like chickens
and pulled away the thin paper of their last days,
pale winegold, a silken globe, pungent,
striped with the pale longitude of silence.

Now over my door they shimmer in knobby garlands,
gregarious in chains like a string of lights
on the boardwalks of heaven where an old man
who loved his garden understands everything.

The Potato Picker

The plant lifts easily now, like an old tooth.
I can free it from the rows of low hills,
hills like the barrows of old kings

where months ago, before anything grew or
    was,
we hid the far-sighted eyes of potatoes.
They fingered forth, blossomed, and shrank,

and did their dark business under our feet.
And now it's all over. Horse nettles dangle
their gold berries. Sunflowers, kindly giants

in their death-rattle turn stiff as streetlamps.
Pale cucumbers swell to alabaster lungs,
while marigolds caught in the quick frost

go brown, and the scarred ears of corn
      gnawed
by the deer lie scattered like primitive fish.
The life boats lifted by milkweed ride light

and empty, their sailors flying.
This is the spot. I put down my spade,
I dig in, I uncover the scraped knees

of children in the village of potatoes,
and the bald heads of their grandfathers.
I enter the potato mines.

Roots

This squash is my good cousin,
says the vegetable man,
rolling his pushcart through November.

These parsnips are first class.
I recommend with my whole heart.
I know the family.

Believe me, lady, I know
what I'm talking.
And I give you a good price.

I throw in the carrots free.
Carrots like this you got?
So what you want?

I wrap in the best Yiddish newspaper.
A dollar a year. Takes me
ten minutes to read it,

an hour to read the English.
Potatoes you need, maybe?
My wife says I eat too many

potatoes. In Poland, in war,
we ate potatoes, soup,
baked, boiled.

All my family was ploughed under
except me. So what can I say
to someone that he don't like

potatoes? Positively last chance,
because tomorrow it might snow.
In winter I don't come.

Look for me when the snow goes,
and if I don't come back,
think that I moved, maybe.

I'm eighty-two already,
and what is Paradise
without such potatoes?

How the Hen Sold Her Eggs
to the Stingy Priest

An egg is a grand thing for a journey.

It will make you a small meal on the road
and a shape most serviceable to the hand

for darning socks, and for barter
a purse of gold opens doors anywhere.

If I wished for a world better than this one
I would keep, in an egg till it was wanted,

the gold earth floating on a clear sea.
If I wished for an angel, that would be my way,

the wings in gold waiting to wake,
the feet in gold waiting to walk,

and the heart that no one believed in
beating and beating the gold alive.

A Wreath to the Fish

Who is this fish, still wearing its wealth,
flat on my drainboard, dead asleep,
its suit of mail proof only against the stream?
What is it to live in a stream,
to dwell forever in a tunnel of cold,
never to leave your shining birthsuit,
never to spend your inheritance of thin coins?
And who is the stream, who lolls all day
in an unmade bed, living on nothing but weather,
singing, a little mad in the head,
opening her apron to shells, carcasses, crabs,
eyeglasses, the lines of fishermen begging for
news from the interior—oh, who are these lines
that link a big sky to a small stream
that go down for great things:
the cold muscle of the trout,
the shining scrawl of the eel in a difficult passage,
hooked—but who is this hook, this cunning
and faithful fanatic who will not let go
but holds the false bait and the true worm alike
and tears the fish, yet gives it up to the basket
in which it will ride to the kitchen
of someone important, perhaps the Pope
who rejoices that his cook has found such a fish
and blesses it and eats it and rises, saying,
"Children, what is it to live in the stream,
day after day, and come at last to the table,
transfigured with spices and herbs,
a little martyr, a little miracle;
children, children, who is this fish?"

A Humane Society

If they don't take animals,
I cannot possibly stay at the Statler
no matter how broad the beds
nor how excellent the view.
Not even if the faucets run hot and cold pearls,
not even if the sheets are cloth of gold,

because I never go anywhere without my raccoon,
my blue raccoon in his nifty mask,
the shadow cast by mind over sight.
I never go abroad without consulting his paw
or reading the weather in the whites of his eyes.
I would share my last crust with his wise mouth.

And even if the manager promised
provisions could be made for a blue raccoon,
I cannot possibly stay at the Waldorf,
no matter how many angels feather the fondues,
no matter how many bishops have blessed the soup,
because I never go anywhere without my cat,

my fuchsia cat in her choirboy bow,
in the purity of whose sleep a nun would feel shamed,
in whose dreams the mouse lies down with the elephant.
I never go to bed without setting her at the door
for her sleep robs even the serpent of poison
and no door closes where she takes her rest,

but even if the manager said, very well,
we can accommodate, for a fee, a fuchsia cat,
I cannot possibly stay at the Ritz.
I understand bears are not welcome there.
I understand that everyone walks on two legs,
and I never go anywhere without my bear

who is comelier of gait than any woman,
who wears no shoes and uses no speech

but many a day has laid down his life for me
in this city of purses, assassins, and the poor.
He would give me his coat and walk abroad in his bones,
and he loves a sunny window and a kind face.

I need a simple room papered with voices
and sorrows without circumstance, and an old lady
in the kitchen below who has welcomed
visitors more desperate than ourselves
and who fondly recalls a pregnant woman riding a donkey
and three crazy men whose only map was a star.

Marriage Amulet

You are polishing me like old wood.
At night we curl together like two rings
on a dark hand. After many nights,
the rough edges wear down.

If this is aging, it is warm as fleece.
I will gleam like ancient wood.
I will wax smooth, my crags and cowlicks
well-rubbed to show my grain.

Some sage will keep us in his hand for peace.

For You, Who Didn't Know

At four A.M. I dreamed myself on that beach
where we'll take you after you're born.
I woke in a wave of blood.

Lying in the back seat of a nervous Chevy
I counted the traffic lights, lonely as planets.
Starlings stirred in the robes of Justice

over the Town Hall. Miscarriage of justice,
they sang, while you, my small client,
went curling away like smoke under my ribs.

Kick me! I pleaded. Give me a sign
that you're still there!
Train tracks shook our flesh from our bones.

Behind the hospital rose a tree of heaven.
        You can learn something from everything,
        a rabbi told his Hasidim who did not believe it.

        I didn't believe it, either. O rabbi,
        what did you learn on the train to Belsen?
        That because of one second one can miss everything.

There are rooms on this earth for emergencies.
A sleepy attendant steals my clothes and my name,
and leaves me among the sinks on an altar of fear.

"Your name. Your name. Sign these papers,
authorizing us in our wisdom to save the child.
Sign here for circumcision. Your faith, your faith."

        O rabbi, what can we learn from the telegraph?
        asked the Hasidim, who did not understand.
        And he answered, *That every word is counted and charged.*

"This is called a dobtone," smiles the doctor.
He greases my belly, stretched like a drum,
and plants a microphone there, like a flag.

A thousand thumping rabbits! Savages clapping for joy!
A heart dancing its name, I'm-here, I'm-here!
The cries of fishes, of stars, the tunings of hair!

O rabbi, what can we learn from a telephone?
My shiksa daughter, your faith, your faith
that what we say here is heard there.

In Praise of ABC

In the beginning were the letters,
wooden, awkward, and everywhere.
Before the Word was the slow scrabble of fire and water.

God bless my son and his wooden letters
who has gone to bed with A in his right hand and Z in his left,
who has walked all day with C in his shoe and said nothing,
who has eaten of his napkin the word Birthday,
and who has filled my house with the broken speech of wizards.

To him the grass makes its gentle sign.
For him the worm letters her gospel truth.
To him the pretzel says, I am the occult
descendant of the first blessed bread
and the lost cuneiform of a grain of wheat.

Kneading bread, I found in my kitchen half an O.
Now I wait for someone to come from far off
holding the other half, saying,
What is broken shall be made whole.
Match half for half; now do you know me again?

Thanks be to God for my house seeded with dark sayings
and my rooms rumpled and badly lit
but richly lettered with the secret raisins of truth.

Walking Poem

How beautifully the child I carry on my back
teaches me to become a horse.
How quickly I learn to stay
between shafts, blinders, and whips,
bearing the plough

and the wagon loaded with hay,
or to break out of trot and run
till we're flying through cold streams.
He who kicks my commands
know I am ten times his size

and that I am servant to small hands.
It is in mowed fields I move best,
watching the barn grow toward me,
the child quiet, his sleep piled like hay
on my back as we slip over the dark hill

and I carry the sun away.

Angels in Winter

Mercy is whiter than laundry,
great baskets of it, piled like snowmen.
In the cellar I fold and sort and watch
through a squint in the dirty window
the plain bright snow.

Unlike the earth, snow is neuter.
Unlike the moon, it stays.
It falls, not from grace, but a silence
which nourishes crystals.
My son catches them on his tongue.

Whatever I try to hold perishes.
My son and I lie down in white pastures
of snow and flap like the last survivors
of a species that couldn't adapt to the air.
Jumping free, we look back at

angels, blurred fossils of majesty and justice
from the time when a ladder of angels
joined the house of the snow
to the houses of those whom it covered
with a dangerous blanket or a healing sleep.

As I lift my body from the angel's,
I remember the mad preacher of Indiana
who chose for the site of his kingdom
the footprint of an angel and named the place
New Harmony. Nothing of it survives.

The angels do not look back
to see how their passing changes the earth,
the way I do, watching the snow,
and the waffles our boots print on its unleavened face,
and the nervous alphabet of the pheasant's feet,

and the five-petaled footprint of the cat,
and the shape of snowshoes, white and expensive as tennis,
and the deep ribbons tied and untied by sleds.
I remember the millions who left the earth;
it holds no trace of them,

as it holds of us, tracking through snow,
so tame and defenseless
even the air could kill us.

Carpenter of the Sun

My child goes forth to fix the sun,
a hammer in his hand and a pocketful of nails.
Nobody else has noticed the crack.

Twilight breaks on the kitchen floor.
His hands clip and hammer the air.
He pulls something out,

something small, like a bad tooth,
and he puts something back,
and the kitchen is full of peace.

All this is done very quietly,
without payment or promises.

One for the Road

On the old bicycle the plumber brought me
Saint Christopher gleams by the traffic bell.
"Good as new." He tapped a rusty fender.
"The girl who rode it moved to Florida.
She was some kind of teacher, too," he grinned.

No baskets, saddlebags, license, or lights.
Eight novels crammed into my backpack—
excessive as a life vest stuffed with stones—
I pedal two miles to the travel agent
to pay for my son's airline ticket home.

Twenty years ago I jogged to market
bearing the light burden of him, bobbing
against my back. Singing to rooks and jays,
he dipped his head under the sky's wing.
He was lighter than my dictionary.

On the threshold, when I set him down,
my muscles quivered, light flooded my bones.
I was a still lake holding up the sky.
Now in his empty room, I hang the map
that flopped out of the *National Geographic*.

Start with what you know, I tell my students.
Detroit, New York, Ann Arbor, Battle Creek—
the roads that spider off from towns I know
are red as arteries that serve the heart
and bring fresh news to all its distant cities,

Madison, Minneapolis–St. Paul.
At his first solo flight away from home
wearing the new jeans he'd bought for school,
his father gave him a gold medal. "Given
for good conduct all the years we had you,

and for good luck." A talisman, a blessing,
friendly as butter: Christopher, untarnished,
bearing the magic child across the stream.

Little Elegy with Books and Beasts

in memory of Martin Provensen (1916–1987)

I

Winters when the gosling froze to its nest
he'd warm it and carry it into the house praising
its finely engraved wings and ridiculous beak—
or sit all night by the roan mare, wrapping
her bruised leg, rinsing the cloths while his wife
read aloud from *Don Quixote*, and darkness hung
on the cold steam of her breath—
or spend five days laying a ladder for the hen
to walk dryshod into the barn.

Now the black cat broods on the porch.
Now the spotted hound meeting visitors, greets none.
Nestler, nurse, mender of wounded things,
he said he didn't believe in the body.
He lost the gander—elder of all their beasts
(not as wise as the cat but more beloved)—
the night of the first frost, the wild geese
calling—last seen waddling south
on the highway, beating his clipped wings.

II

He stepped outside through the usual door
and saw for the last time his bare maples
scrawling their cold script on the low hills
and the sycamore mottled as old stone
and the willows slurred into gold by the spring light,
and he noticed the boy clearing the dead brush—
old boughs that broke free under the cover of snow,
and he raised his hand, and a door in the air opened,
and what was left of him stumbled and fell
and lay at rest on the earth like a clay lamp
still warm whose flame was not nipped or blown
but lifted out by the one who lit it
and carried alive over the meadow—
that light by which we read, while he was here,
the chapter called Joy in the Book of Creation.

The Poet Invites the Moon for Supper

Tonight a stranger followed me home.
He wore an overcoat and feathers.
His head was as light as summer.
When I saw how much light he spilled
on the street, I knew he was rich.

He wanted to make me his heir.
I said, no thank you, I have a father.
He wanted to give me the snow to wife.
I said, no thank you, I have a sweetheart.
He wanted to make me immortal.
And I said, no thank you, but when you see
somebody putting me into the mouth
of the earth, don't fret.
I am a song.
Someone is writing me down.
I am disappearing into the ear of a rose.

The Poet Takes a Photograph
of His Heart

The doctor told him,
Something is living in your heart.
The poet borrowed a camera.
He told his heart to smile.
He slipped the plate under his ribs
and caught his heart running out of the picture.
He told his heart to relax.
It beat on the plate with its fist.
It did not want to lose its face!
He told his heart he was taking nothing
but an ikon by which to remember it.
Then the heart stood up like a bandstand
and the wren who lived under the eaves
left her nest and started
the long journey south.

The Poet Turns His Enemy
into a Pair of Wings

His enemy was a dragon laced with medals.
It picked his pockets, hid his poems,
beat its tail on his head at night,
blew the nose off his wife's face.
For God's sake, peace! cried the poet.
Then the dragon jumped on his back.
Warm in his lizardskin coat he stepped outside.
No one, no one else in the snowy city
wore a lizardskin coat!
Its purple hearts jingled like temple bells.
It rested its pointed chin on the poet's head.
Go right, said the dragon.
The poet skipped left.
Go up, said the dragon.
The poet went downtown.
At one o'clock it turned yellow.
At two o'clock it turned green.
Go up, said the dragon, or let me be.
I am Salamander, fireman of the stars,
bound to cross my brow with their ashes.
How shall I go? asked the poet.
Just as you are, said the dragon,
day in night, night in hand,
hand in pocket, pocket in poem,
poem in bone, bone in flesh,
flesh in flight.

The Poet's Wife Watches Him
Enter the Eye of the Snow

She knew he was writing a poem
because everything in the room
was slowly sifting away:
her dustpan the color of buttercups,
her eyeglasses and her sink
and her five masks praising the sun.

That night she saw him ascend.
He floated above their bed,
he gathered the dark strands
of the poem like a tide.

On his nose her glasses polished
themselves to crystals. On his back
the dustpan fanned out
like a saffron cape.
Now he was turning his face toward the sun
and riding her simple sink into heaven.

In the morning she calls to the newsboy:
"How can I, wife of the poet,
know what he saw and did there?
It is enough that I open my eyes

and my glasses perch on my nose
and show me the brittle dreams of parrots.
Enough that my dustpan believes it shoulders
the broken bones of those warriors the stars,
that my sink gurgles for joy,
and my five masks tell me more
than I knew when I made them."

The Ballad of Biddy Early

"I've an empty stomach,
you've an empty purse.
You feel your fingers freezing?
Outside it's ten times worse,
so listen to my story.
Forget the wind and rain.
It's time for bed," the tinker said,
"but pass the cup again.

"I sing of Biddy Early,
the wise woman of Clare.
Many's the man admires her
carrot-colored hair,
and many those that come to her
on horseback or by cart,
for she can heal a broken leg
or a broken heart.

"She keeps a magic bottle
in whose majestic eye
a tiny coffin twinkles
and if it sinks, you die.
It rises, you grow better
and slip out of your pain.
It's time for bed," the tinker said,
"but pass the cup again.

"She covers the great bottle
and runs to fetch the small,
filled with a bright elixir,
honey and sage and gall.
She'll take no gold or silver
but maybe a speckled hen.
It's time for bed," the tinker said.
"Let's pass the cup again.

"*Follow the stream,* she told me.
Go where the salmon goes.
Avoid mischievous bridges
for even water knows
if you should drop this bottle—"
He turned and spoke no more.
Biddy Early's shadow
was listening at the door.

How the Magic Bottle Gave
Biddy Its Blessing

"Sighing stones, ghosts and bones,
and who will dig a grave
for roaring Tom, that bloody man
who with a pistol gave
death to seven people?
The gravediggers have fled.
So let the lightning bury him,"
the deathwatch bettle said.

"Even the wicked need a grave
and it's a dreadful thing
for any man to make his bed
under the vulture's wing.
Give me the spade and pickax.
A murderer who's dead
can do no harm to anyone,"
Biddy Early said.

She sank her spade into the sod—
the stones began to weep.
"The little mice," said Biddy,
"are singing in their sleep."
She sank her spade into the roots—
their cry turned her to ice.
The deathwatch beetle snickered,
"An owl has caught the mice."

Six feet down in darkness
she heard the shovel chime
against an old blue bottle
glittering under grime.
With sleeve and spit she polished it
and heard the bottle call,
"Of all things born at midnight
I am most magical.

"Nothing known shall come to pass,
no secret word or wish,
that I have not reflected.
Bird, beast, or fish,
every living thing shall praise
the healing in your hand,
Biddy, the bravest woman
in all of Ireland."

Charm of the Gold Road, the Silver Road, and the Hidden Road

On my thumb
I spun
two roads
from one thread,
half silver,
half gold.
I made them
and laid them
over the land
and said,

"May those who follow you
find gold but not glowworms,
coins but not crickets,
treasure but not tree toads,
silver but not silence,
money but not moonlight,
                    not magic,

            and not me."

How the Queen of the Gypsies
Met Trouble-and-Pain

My name is Maureen, I'm the tinker-town queen.
My caravan travels from Gort to Kildare.
When my pony went lame, I remembered the fame
of Biddy the healer, wise woman of Clare.
Bright star of the morning, she gave me fair warning:
"Under my bridge huddles Trouble-and-Pain.
For the sake of this bottle, the creature will throttle
both you and your horse as you cross its domain."

I gave her a ring, hammered out like a wing,
I gave her green ribbons to tie up her hair,
a velveteen fan, and a new frying pan
and left with her blessing for Limerick Fair.
When we came to the bridge, my horse wouldn't budge.
The bottle grew frightened, it trembled and sighed,
and the harder I held it, the stronger I felt it:
a ghostly hand grappled, a ghostly mouth cried,

"May your horse never walk, may your son never talk.
May the saber-toothed gnats make a nest in your hair.
May your logs never burn, may your dog never learn,
and your purse turn to feathers at Limerick Fair.
May your buttermilk bark, may your lanterns go dark,
and your skillets and petticoats take to the air.
May you drown in the lake, unless I can take
that bottle of Biddy's, wise woman of Clare."

When it reared up its head, I took courage and said,
"By my mother's gold tooth and my father's glass eye—"
Then down the bridge clattered, the bottle was shattered,
but Trouble-and-Pain was more frightened than I.
Some say life is brief as the fall of a leaf,
and nothing lives long that lives under the sun,
but friends and relations in five gypsy nations
shall whisper my story till stories are done.

38

How Biddy Hid Mick the Moonlighter's Sleep in Her Sleeve

Mick came to her house at midnight
and pounded on Biddy's door.
"I have murdered William O'Sheehy
for sucking the blood from the poor.

"He put me out of my cottage,
he burned my house to the ground.
I have murdered William O'Sheehy
and will hang for it, if I am found."

Biddy spoke to her magic bottle,
she held it against her ear
and heard O'Sheehy's men riding
and whispered, "Go far from here.

"Take the little road to Liscanoor.
Speak to nobody on the way.
Take the broken dinghy to Kilrush
and a ship to Amerikay."

Mick wrote a name in the ashes
while the moon looked in at the door.
"Before I go, Biddy darling,
will you help me one time more?

"Will you tell the murdered man's sister
I'm wanted dead or alive,
and if she'll follow a wanted man
I'll send for her when I arrive?"

Biddy spoke to her magic bottle,
and the woods and the roads fell asleep,
the tinkers and turnips and mill wheels,
the soldiers and salmon and sheep.

Mick the Moonlighter's weariness left him.
It circled O'Sheehy's land
and darted through Biddy's window
and settled on Biddy's hand.

She folded its wings with a promise,
she stroked its breast with a sigh,
she made it a nest in her right sleeve
and closed its wicked green eye.

Not a soul stirred or wakened
from Feakle to Usher's Well.
O'Sheehy's men came in the morning,
saying, "Tell, tell."

"The bird has flown," said Biddy,
"where the moon and the stars run free.
The man you seek is fast asleep,
safe on the Irish Sea."

Biddy Early Makes a Long Story Short

I, Biddy Early, come from the Red Hills.
My mother traveled under the cold sky
and carried me, her firstborn, on her back.
May the roads she walked stay with me till I die.

I am at home with hunger. For my bread
I learned to haul stones, scrub floors, and cook.
When Mother died, a wren taught me to read
the spells in streams and stones. Earth was my book.

The priest tells me, "Biddy, come to Mass."
I say, "Father, when I kneel down alone
the people whisper things. I want to live
out of their sight, with crickets and cats and stones,

"and when I die, I shall give back to Earth
all her gifts for the healing of hurts and ills.
I shall come back in water and words and leaves,
I, Biddy Early, asleep in the Red Hills."

Song from the Far Side of Sleep

Lullaby, my little cat,
Lord of Mouse and Knave of Bat.
Hail, Mischief, full of grace,
who did lately love this place.

Lullaby your crescent claws
in the chambers of your paws,
which you sharpen day and night,
keeping all my kettles bright.

Lullaby your gentle purr.
What small spirits did you lure
to the mushroom rings I made
and the lesser spells we laid?

Lullaby your pebbled tongue.
Keep my velvets every young.
Keep my slippers ever slick
with the patience of a lick.

Lullaby your lively tail.
Never have I seen it fail,
spirits gone and revels done,
to point the quickest highway home.

Eternal life, eternal death
hang on our Creator's breath.
Little tiger in God's eye,
remember Biddy's lullaby.

William Blake's Inn for Innocent and Experienced Travelers

This inn belongs to William Blake
and many are the beasts he's tamed
and many are the stars he's named
and many those who stop and take
their joyful rest with William Blake.

Two mighty dragons brew and bake
and many are the loaves they've burned
and many are the spits they've turned
and many those who stop and break
their joyful bread with William Blake.

Two patient angels wash and shake
his featherbeds, and far away
snow falls like feathers. That's the day
good children run outside and make
snowmen to honor William Blake.

Blake Leads a Walk on the Milky Way

He gave silver shoes to the rabbit
and golden gloves to the cat
and emerald boots to the tiger and me
and boots of iron to the rat.

He inquired, "Is everyone ready?
The night is uncommonly cold.
We'll start on our journey as children,
but I fear we will finish it old."

He hurried us to the horizon
where morning and evening meet.
The slippery stars went skipping
under our hapless feet.

"I'm terribly cold," said the rabbit.
"My paws are becoming quite blue,
and what will become of my right thumb
while you admire the view?"

"The stars," said the cat, "are abundant
and falling on every side.
Let them carry us back to our comforts.
Let us take the stars for a ride."

"I shall garland my room," said the tiger,
"with a few of these emerald lights."
"I shall give up sleeping forever," I said.
"I shall never part day from night."

The rat was sullen. He grumbled
he ought to have stayed in his bed.
"What's gathered by fools in heaven
will never endure," he said.

Blake gave silver stars to the rabbit
and golden stars to the cat
and emerald stars to the tiger and me
but a handful of dirt to the rat.

The King of Cats
Sends a Postcard to His Wife

Keep your whiskers crisp and clean.
Do not let the mice grow lean.
Do not let yourself grow fat
like a common kitchen cat.

Have you set the kittens free?
Do they sometimes ask for me?
Is our catnip growing tall?
Did you patch the garden wall?

Clouds are gentle walls that hide
gardens on the other side.
Tell the tabby cats I take
all my meals with William Blake,

lunch at noon and tea at four,
served in splendor on the shore
at the tinkling of a bell.
Tell them I am sleeping well.

Tell them I have come so far,
brought by Blake's celestial car,
buffeted by wind and rain,
I may not get home again.

Take this message to my friends.
Say the King of Catnip sends
to the cat who winds his clocks
a thousand sunsets in a box,

to the cat who brings the ice
the shadows of a dozen mice
(serve them with assorted dips
and eat them like potato chips),

and to the cat who guards his door
a net for catching stars, and more
(if with patience he abide):
catnip from the other side.

The Tiger Asks Blake for a Bedtime Story

William, William, writing late
by the chill and sooty grate,
what immortal story can
make your tiger roar again?

When I was sent to fetch your meat
I confess that I did eat
half the roast and all the bread.
He will never know, I said.

When I was sent to fetch your drink,
I confess that I did think
you would never miss the three
lumps of sugar by your tea.

Soon I saw my health decline
and I knew the fault was mine.
Only William Blake can tell
tales to make a tiger well.

Now I lay me down to sleep
with bear and rabbit, bird and sheep.
If I should dream before I wake,
may I dream of William Blake.

Epilogue

My adventures now are ended.
I and all whom I befriended
from this holy hill must go
home to lives we left below.

Farewell cow and farewell cat,
rabbit, tiger, sullen rat.
To our children we shall say
how we walked the Milky Way.

You whose journeys now begin,
if you reach a lovely inn,
if a rabbit makes your bed,
if two dragons bake your bread,
rest a little for my sake,
and give my love to William Blake.

"Buffalo Climbs Out of Cellar"

"Will you have some sherry?" asked
the million-dollar baby-faced killer.

He filled my glass, and the whole room
sucked me into its sharkish smile.

"You're fond of hunting," I said.
"Did you shoot all those guys on the wall?"

He nodded and raised the cuff of his pants.
His left leg was ivory to the knee.

"That Bengal tiger was my first success.
Then I matched wits with a white whale

and won. After that I went in for elephants.
And then I heard about the last buffalo

in South Dakota. Very educated.
He speaks fluent Apache. He writes

by scratching his hooves in the dirt.
He's writing a history of the Civil War.

So naturally I took him alive. Day
and night I keep him locked in my cellar.

His breath heats this house all winter.
His heart charges all my rooms with light.

In my worst dreams I see them folding up
like a paper hat, and my dead tiger roaring

and my dead whale swimming off the wall
and my buffalo climbing out of the cellar."

"Saints Lose Back"

And there was complacency in heaven
for the space of half an hour,
and God said, Let every saint lose his back.

Let their wings and epaulettes shrivel,
and for immortal flesh give them flesh of man,
and for the wind of heaven a winter on earth.

The saints roared like the devil.
O my God, cried Peter, what have you done?
And God said,

Consider the back,
the curse of backache
the humpback's prayer.

Consider how thin a shell man wears.
The locust and crab are stronger than he.
Consider the back, how a rod breaks it.

Now consider the front, adorned with eyes,
cheeks, lips, breasts, all
the gorgeous weaponry of love.

Then consider the back, good for nothing
but to fetch and carry, crouch and bear
and finally to lie down on the earth.

O, my angels, my exalted ones,
consider the back,
consider how the other half lives.

"Divine Child Rolls On"

Lullaby, my sparrow.
Cipher, make your mark
in the Book of Being.
Fly into the dark,

passenger of the planet.
Sun and stars are gone.
The Divine Child find you,
bless you, and roll on.

The Hucklebone of a Saint

I N   M Y   father's house, moral ambiguity was not allowed. It was considered unhealthy, like soft drinks and candy, not to be kept in the house and to be eaten only with reprimands that kept you from enjoying it. As a result of this stricture, until I was ten, my father and I saw little of each other. We had a nodding acquaintance at meals, during which he listened to the news on the radio and spoke to no one. When I heard his car crunching up the driveway at night, bringing him back from the laboratory where he worked both morning and evening, I knew I should be asleep.

It was my mother who gave me my faith in the black arts, which came to dire fruition in my tenth year. Faith takes root in the insignificant. We would be sitting around the dinner table and I would drop my knife.

"Pick it up, Erica," my father would say. Or perhaps he would say nothing, but I would feel a discomforting frown.

"A man is coming," my mother would add.

Or if I dropped a spoon:

"A child is coming."

I never thought to notice whether or not the prophecies came true. I only remembered that if you dropped a knife, a man would visit the house for certain. Not that day, perhaps, nor the next, but sometime when you did not expect it. When you had even forgotten you dropped the knife.

My father did not recognize the power of a knife to bring a visitor, any more than he recognized the power of an umbrella opened indoors to bring bad luck. Knowing that differences exist most peacefully under one roof when they are unaware of each other, my mother did not practice her black arts openly before him. If she knocked over the saltcellar while clearing the table, she brushed a small pile

55

of salt aside and waited till he was napping before she threw a pinch of it into the fire. She knew he would ask, just as I asked, and he would be harder to answer:

"Why?"

"Judas spilled salt at the Last Supper. And look what happened to him."

I had seen da Vinci's *Last Supper* hanging like an enormous postcard in the Sunday School parlor of the Lutheran Church, and I resolved to look for the salt.

"See for yourself. It's lying on the table by Judas's hand, just like it's lying on our table now."

"But just because Judas had bad luck, why should I have it?"

"Just because."

Not because one man, this particular man had had it, certainly. The more I thought about it, the more I knew I could not inherit Judas's bad luck the way you inherit the color of your eyes and the shape of your face. Rather, in spilling the salt he had somehow stumbled upon a law. Others had probably discovered it before him. But it took the Crucifixion and Potter's Field before its validity was recognized.

It occurred to me that there must be many such laws I did not know. It had never worried me before. I knew it was my father's business to find out the laws which kept the world running. When he took me to the laboratory with him, I saw that it was full of things whose secrets he was wresting.

"What are those pretty stones?"

"Those are minerals."

"Why do you keep them in that funny box?"

"Because they're radioactive."

It was his pleasure to open the laws that lay hidden in things and make them clear, so clear that I could touch them with my hands whenever I picked up the models of molecular structures he kept in a little glass case on his desk. What he found was beautiful and utterly irrelevant to the way I lived my life. The world would go on turning whether my father or anyone else's father found out why. To discover the law of gravity, for example, was only to name what you already knew. It didn't change a thing.

The uselessness of my father's laws made them easier to learn than my mother's. He had marvelous instruments to extend the range of the senses and reach into the very cells of being. And when you found one law, you found others contingent on it. Whereas the laws in my mother's world were utterly capricious. You stepped on a crack and if your mother's back broke, you knew you'd found the reason. There were no conclusions, only an infinite number of particular cases.

And knowing the laws that worked in particular cases did not free you from the fear of breaking them. It only committed you more deeply to a power that gave you nothing in return for your obedience, except the vague feeling that you were somehow maintaining the status quo.

As soon as I acknowledged the existence of my mother's laws, life became immensely more complicated. Since each law was a particular event, the smallest events suggested themselves as a possible means of discovery. Riding my bicycle, for example, I would innocently imagine that if the stoplight turned red before I reached it, something bad would happen. If it didn't, things would stay the same. Nothing good would happen, but nothing bad would, either. Once I had decided it might be so, the game became real. The stoplight had the power to direct the traffic of my future. I began to avoid stoplights.

Other events acquired a similar authority which had to be countered with rituals and taboos. Certain dresses brought bad luck and hung unworn in the closet. Tuesdays meant low marks on spelling quizzes and mistakes in mathematics.

The most discouraging part of the whole business was that it was so much easier to bring bad luck on oneself than good luck. It was so much easier to break a mirror and live in the shadow of impending misfortune than to count a hundred white horses and wish for happiness.

As the games I invented mysteriously turned into statutes, I believed that I was maintaining the even keel of our joys until one day I came home from school to find two suitcases in the front hall. Grandmother had left her husband and decided to live with us.

She was to live out her life in our guest room, which quickly took on the color and smell of her life. It was a cold room, shut off from the house, with a pink satin bolster on the bed and doilies on the dressing table and a clean blotter on the desk; one of those anonymous rooms often slept in and rarely lived in, like a room in a hotel. Now the bolster gave way to a dozen eiderdowns. The radiators clanked and pounded; the room was kept at eighty degrees. My grandmother went about in heavy underclothes and sweaters and seldom left her quarters for more tepid parts of the house.

Further, its innocent spaces were suddenly thronged with medicine bottles of all kinds: lecithin, calcium, supplementary organic pills, Kaopectate, and Hexylresorcinol. There were also cases of vitamins, each regulating some function of the body and therefore necessary—Grandmother believed—to its survival. In her suitcase, which I observed was never wholly unpacked, she kept a reserve supply of everything.

On the wall over the bed hung a Chinese painting of a mountain. This she disliked, though she never asked us to take it down.

"Mountains! What good are mountains? You can't farm land like that."

Her chief amusement was going to church. She listened to the sermon with great attentiveness but could never remember a word of it afterward. She enjoyed the music and the feeling of being united with so many people for the good of their souls, which she had been taught was the only good.

She passed her days with what I considered an unbearable monotony. In the morning my mother brought up her oatmeal and orange juice on a tray. Grandmother sat at the dressing table and ate in front of the mirror, while my mother combed her long white hair into two braids and pinned them crosswise on her head. Then my mother went down to the cellar to hang up the wash—for it was early April when my grandmother came, and too cold to hang clothes outside—always listening for the sound of the old woman's voice.

"Daughter?"

"I'm right here."

Assured she was not alone, Grandmother would set about arranging the accoutrements of her life—that is, the contents of the suitcase. In addition to her impressive collection of medicines, she kept extra sets of heavy underwear and rolls of toilet paper which she sometimes unwound and wadded into her garters like an amulet to ward off attacks of nervous diarrhea.

It seemed to me that she was pursuing a secret journey, the destination of which constantly evaded her. Sometimes she would come to lunch wearing her hat and her big sealskin coat, inquiring about bus schedules, hinting that she had not been well treated. My mother's response was always the same.

"There are no buses today. It's a holiday."

"Ah, then, I'll have to wait."

Then she would mention her responsibilities at the house in Coronna which she had so recently left and where my mother had grown up. Men were coming to pick the cherries in the orchard; she had to look sharp that they did not cheat on the hours. Grandfather was waiting for her; who would fix his dinner? She would explain it to us with pathetic urgency.

My mother maintained the illusion through a round of outings which never got the woman to her destination but only postponed the total collapse of her reason.

Grandmother's favorite escort on these outings was her brother Oskar. He was seventy-one, seven years younger than my grandmother. To me he was ageless, a spry, dapper little man who always wore two-toned Oxfords and a black and yellow vest, giving him the look of a frail and friendly bee. He was retired, not from any single occupation but from a great variety of them, including brief stints as homesteader, circus barker, undertaker's assistant, and shortstop for an obscure ball team in Minnesota. He had once had a wife and child, both of whom were dead, and I remember neither.

Sometimes he wrote poems—jingles, he called them—on the placemats he got every noon at Howard Johnson's, surfaces as suggestive to him as marble to Michelangelo, their floral borders and bright colors concealing clusters of language. Slipping a finely folded jingle into my hand, he would greet me with a mock bow, his shoes twinkling.

"Ah, Miss Callard," he would say.

"Oh, Bowser, how I've missed you."

That was in honor of the candies he kept in his pockets, Callard and Bowser's Plain Jane Toffees, or Lady Fingers, or Licorice. If he had no candy, then I knew he was bringing a game, a card trick, perhaps, or a Cracker-Jack toy. My mother justified his passion for Cracker Jacks by saying they reminded him of baseball, but I could see well enough how he broke into smiles of satisfaction when the toy appeared at the bottom of the box. Of all his presents he said, with a mixture of shame and pride,

59

"It's nothing; I got it for pennies."

He would drive Grandmother around town to parade, as he called it, in my father's car. Sometimes I went along, sitting alone in the backseat.

"You want to take the wheel, my girl?" he suggested, turning solemnly to his sister.

Grandmother looked at him with horror.

"You used to do very well. I remember how we had the only car in Deep River, and how you used to make me get out at every corner and look in all directions to see if another one was coming."

. Her early scruples eventually overcame her, for when my mother was fourteen, Grandmother drove the car into the garage and forgot to take it out again. No one else in the family had a license, so there it remained while my grandmother thought of more and more reasons for walking to this place and that, until it was understood that the car was now part of the house, as immovable as the walls and the floor.

On Sundays, my great-uncle came for breakfast, bringing with him a small flute of his own carving. He never went with us to church but waited at the house to join us for dinner, after which he retired to the sun room for a nap. He slept with his eyes open for about an hour and then I would hear him talking to the flute, as if he had no idea of gaining my audience.

"There was an organ in the house where we grew up. All the German farmhouses had them. Your grandmother used to sit in the parlor and play it by the hour."

"Where is it now?" I had always wanted to play an organ but thought that all organs were indissolubly joined to churches.

Oskar shook his head.

"The spitzwinks took it."

It was the German farmers in Iowa who told Oskar about the spitzwinks. Sometimes the crops failed because of rain, sometimes because of drought. And sometimes they failed for no reason at all. Then the farmers said, "Ah, the spitzwinks have done it." The spitzwinks made holes in your best stockings and chipped the cups and saucers that you used every day. They were the reason that plants marked "annuals" on the box at the market would not return in the spring.

"But why didn't Great-Grandpa lock up the organ so the spitzwinks wouldn't steal it? Didn't he know there'd be other children?"

"He never thought of it."

The spitzwinks, I thought, were a sort of game, with no more substance than a figure of speech. But as weeks turned into months and Grandmother stayed on, I soon saw them as a name for forces which enmeshed her in propitiatory rituals far more suffocating than my own.

When she was dressed for bed and had drunk the hot milk that my mother brought her, she closed her door and began the long process of barricading it. Lying in my bed I could hear the moving of furniture, the heaviest pieces in the house and a chilling testimony of my grandmother's strength. A long slow scraping across the floor was the chest of drawers. Then came the slow bump of the dressing table with the oval mirror. That did not move so easily because the castors had disappeared. And finally I heard a persistent scuffling sound, as if my grandmother were waging a battle with the forces of darkness. In half an hour the sounds ceased but the light still shone under her door; she was awake.

"Margaret, did you lock the front door?"

That was my mother, who always sounded like somebody else when anyone called her by her first name.

"Yes!" My father was already asleep; he left to my mother the responsibility of answering.

For a few minutes it would be still. Then I heard the furniture moving again, the chest of drawers, the dressing table, the chair. This time, it was being forced away from the door. When the door opened, Grandmother's voice sounded near. She had stepped into the hall.

"I say, did you lock the front door?"

"Yes, of course!"

"I think I'll just go down and try it."

Like the soul of an extinct bird she glided swiftly down the stairs, her two braids springing out over her ears just as they fell when she took out the pins. She rattled the knob of the front door for us all to hear.

"Good. I just wanted to be sure."

Then her own door would slam, as if she had reached her room in a single bound. And presently the moving of furniture would begin again.

Night after night I acknowledged the danger that lay in such defenses. Clearly my grandmother's rituals only brought her closer to the fears she wished to avoid. Mine were still part of the games that a child plays, when by an act of the imagination he wills his own life into what has none, for the sake of companionship. If my grandmother's rituals were a game, then it must be a game that she played in deadly earnest, the stakes to be paid with her own life. Whenever I recognized this, I had the uncomfortable feeling that we were becoming more and more alike.

What linked us was a discovery that the faith we had gathered from generations of Sundays was no match for this greater faith in the reality of darkness. Where did it come from? We had not invited it. Who put it into my heart that the darkness under the bed gathered itself into invisible hands, waiting to snatch my feet when I groped my way back from the bathroom at night? How was it that my mother, my father, and Uncle Oskar stepped quietly into their beds with no knowledge of this danger and therefore no fear? How could you lose your freedom without knowing who had taken it? If my faith in the darkness could not be broken, then it was not faith as I knew it but a love for all that could not be named and a secret desire that it never should be.

Because of this love my mother wore her best dress wrong side out to my cousin's wedding for fear of bringing bad luck on the heads of the newly wedded pair. Because of this love she knocked on wood whenever she spoke of my achievements in school and asserted half-jokingly—but only half—that Thomas Dewey had lost the presidential election because he had a horseshoe hanging upside down over his door and all his luck drained out. She had grown up in a neighboring town and seen for herself the quiet gnawing emblem of his doom which, if heeded, might have changed the course of nations.

By day, Grandmother's diversions alternated between drives, church, and Abby's beauty parlor. The beauty parlor and the church stood kitty corner from each other, on a block named by persecuted German immigrants who wanted their children to grow up on Liberty Street. The slow but ceaseless arrival of new settlers gave it such a vivid restlessness that even now I think of it not as a place but as a way of being alive.

The excitement began early in the morning when men in white

overalls streaked with blood hauled carcasses from trucks to the back of the butcher shop. But when its doors opened for business, the very memory of blood had been quenched. Sausages were hung high on the ceiling, tucked out of sight like poor relations, to be asked for by name but not displayed. On shelves that ran the length of the shop you found cocoa from Holland in delftware jars, flatbread from Norway, and flowered tins of gumdrops from Paris.

Abby had her beauty shop above the butcher's, and it was there that I met Mary Ellen. She was two years older than I and had the job of answering the telephone and unwrapping the little pieces of cotton which Abby tucked into the hairnets of her customers to protect their ears from the sirocco blasts of the dryer. She also kept the glass atomizers filled with the heavy scented lacquer which "set" the finger-waves so that hair came out dry and rippling as dunes of sand.

In exchange for these favors, Abby allowed her to read the movie magazines she kept by the dryers. Mary Ellen devoured the legends of her favorites as faithfully as she attended Mass. The stars were her secular saints, their changeless identities to be consulted in the minute crises of daily life. She borrowed a gesture from one, a hairstyle from another; all, I thought, to no effect. There was a faint aura of dirt about everything she wore, like a shading sketched on the original color, and as she washed the pins and curlers, customers would stare at her fingernails in amazement. For she did not believe in cleaning them; she simply bit the dirty portion away, peeling it with great fastidiousness like a delicate fruit.

In warm weather we walked to a vacant lot behind a funeral parlor, where we could play undisturbed. The only other building on it was a warehouse full of coffins. Squeezing among them like bankers checking their safes, we would collect the number of different kinds, the way you collect out-of-state license plates or the number of white horses you pass when you are traveling. Most of the coffins were dark and plain. We decided it was lucky to find a baby's coffin, because we found them so seldom. A few of the large ones were scrolled, and we watched for these, too, though their luck was considered less potent. At the end of the day we remembered how many we had found.

Or rather *I* remembered how many we had found. I had come to believe that the luck things carried augmented like interest only if I kept my books straight, never forgetting how much I had saved. When the total number of white horses, license plates, loads of hay, baby coffins, and other spectacles deemed lucky by us grew too large to keep in my head, I wrote the sums down in a little notebook, with the conviction that it was both useless and necessary to some final reckoning of my fate.

By this time the last platoon of Abby's customers would be touching their brittle curls as they emerged from under the dryers. Grandmother never sat under the dryer, as it threw her into a panic and she would roll her eyes about like a horse being pushed into a van. With her hair pinned in wet braids across her head, she turned the pages of the movie magazines, clucking at the wages of sin until my mother emerged with her hair pitilessly knotted into ringlets.

"It's so hard to find someone who can do my hair plain the way I like it," she would say.

Abby's hairdos were utterly without style. She believed in durability rather than immediate effect. She made pincurls so tight that they kept their kink for days and only ceased to remind you of sheep's wool or unshorn poodles a week later. On her walls hung photographs showing a wide variety of styles, but no matter which one you ordered you always came out looking the same. This attracted a host of elderly ladies whose conservative taste could not be met in the salons uptown, where ratting and backcombing were the fashion.

Although I knew Abby had been a widow oftener than some wives have been mothers, I could not imagine her in love. She was a stocky figure, in her white smock, with sparse brown hair and thick glasses, and as she tipped your head into the sink and scrubbed your scalp, she sang at the top of her voice:

> "When you're smiling,
> When you're smiling,
> The whole world smiles with you."

And while she sang, always a little breathless from reaching and scrubbing, she talked and talked and her bosom heaved like a full sail over your face. Neither I nor my mother knew any of the people she talked about, except as we might feel we knew the characters in a radio serial—Pearl, Maria, Charley, and all the others whose foibles she expounded to us according to her mood.

"He's gone to see that widow lady downstairs, that's what. He lies around on her bed all day and she feeds him white albacore tuna. It's nothing but grub what he's after, a heartless beast, no feelings at all."

Not for a long time did I learn that many of the names I associated with people actually belonged to cats. Abby fed all the stray cats that came to her door and demanded in exchange a scrupulous fidelity. If one stayed away for two days, or a week, she railed against him like a forsaken lover.

With Grandmother, however, she never spoke of cats. Every conversation was an exchange of ailments and remedies, Grandmother defending her drugstore prescriptions and Abby speaking for her teas. Among her rinses she kept a packet of alba camomile, the label of which showed a man coming out of a forest and handing a spray of blossoms to a little girl. To me, that alone argued for its magical properties.

"Someday you'll be drinking a good dose of henna if you're not careful, keeping it all mixed up like that," warned my mother.

But Abby's cupboard contained a greater wonder than alba camomile tea. It was locked away in a small chest behind the bleaches and dyes. Sometimes, when all her customers were safely tucked under the dryers and time lay heavy on her hands, she would bring it out for Mary Ellen and me to look at.

"It's the hucklebone of a saint," explained Abby.

I did not dare to ask what a hucklebone was and decided that it was the place on your elbow that tingled when you accidentally bumped it against a table or chair. I have since learned that it is the anklebone.

The tiny splinter of bone lay pressed between two discs of glass in the middle of a brass sun from which crude rays emanated. Abby's grandfather, a connoisseur of the marvelous, had bought it in the catacombs outside Rome from a priest who took him through by the light of a serpent twisted around his staff. At Cologne he had kissed the skulls of the Magi and the nail driven into Christ's right foot; at Trèves he had touched part of the thigh of the Virgin Agatha and seen the devil carrying the soul of his grandmother in a wheelbarrow. He had walked on the holy stair of Saint John Lateran and wagered for a tooth of Saint Peter. He lost the wager, but the same day he was miraculously healed of a lifetime of headaches by combing his hair with the comb of a saint.

"Which saint?" asked Mary Ellen.

"I don't know. What does it matter?"

I liked the saints, faded as they were in the liturgies of my church.

I liked them because they attended so patiently to the smallest human catastrophes. If you lost something you went to Saint Anthony. If you wanted a husband you went to Saint Nicholas. Even thieves found a comforter among the ranks of the blessed, who would not turn a deaf ear to their problems.

I had need for such a comforter. Since my grandmother's arrival my dependence on the dark powers had grown steadily worse. I had come to believe that certain words released the forces of evil, being part of that vast body of laws of which spilling salt was only a tiny amendment. All my life, words had come to me wrapped in feelings that had nothing to do with their meanings and everything to do with the way my hand felt when I printed them. But now they lost all connection with the things they named and took on the opacity of a magic formula. Not being able to say *tree* didn't mean that trees were evil. It only meant that saying the name released forces beyond your control.

Perfect obedience led, clearly, to perfect silence, and the slow death of all my delights. You cannot serve two masters. Or rather, you can, but the moment will come when you must choose between them.

We were crossing the lot on our way to the coffins when suddenly Mary Ellen stamped her foot and cried,

"Lucky Strike!"

"What?"

"I stepped on a new one. See?"

So I stepped on it also.

"Lucky Strike."

She shook her head.

"You can say it if you want to, but it isn't as good as if you'd found your own. It counts less. And don't *ever* step on a Pall Mall."

I felt a whole new mesh of complications engulf me.

"Let's not count cigarette packs. It's too hard."

I wanted her to tell me that in the scheme of things, Lucky Strikes and Pall Malls did not matter. Instead, she only looked at me in astonishment.

"Too *hard*?"

"I can't remember so many things." I was beginning to feel irritable. "Why do we have to count things all the time? You keep track of license plates, you keep track of everything."

"It's only a game," she said in puzzled tones.

"Well, it isn't a game to me!" I bellowed.

The door of the funeral parlor opened and a man stepped out and cleared his throat. We scuttled across the lot to the street and began walking quickly past the houses toward downtown.

"A lot of people in there," whispered Mary Ellen, looking back over her shoulder. "You want to watch?"

"I don't want to watch anything anymore! I'm tired of counting. All those things, I *have* to count them. I don't know why but I have to count them. And I don't want to. My head is so crowded with junk already that sometimes I feel like it's going to explode."

"Then why don't you quit?"

"I don't know!" My voice had risen to a shout. An old woman sitting on her front porch stared at us. "It's like there was some other person inside of me making me do it. Every time I want to quit there's that other person who won't let me."

Mary Ellen nodded.

"Somebody has put a hex on you, maybe," she suggested.

"Maybe," I agreed.

"If it happened to *me,* I'd just go straight to Father Hekkel and he would make it all right."

The notion of involving a stranger alarmed me at once. Now that I'd dragged the thing into broad daylight it sounded foolish even to my own ears.

"Since you aren't in our church, maybe Father Hekkel wouldn't work. We better try and find somebody else."

"What about Abby?"

We were lucky. The only customer was white-haired Miss Briggs who worked in a dry goods store and looked like somebody's memory of a piano teacher. Miss Briggs was hunched under the dryer reading a confession magazine with the front cover folded back, and Abby was sweeping up the hair clippings that lay around the chairs into a feathery pile.

Mary Ellen walked in and came right to the point.

"Erica has a devil in her."

"Lord-a-mighty!" cried Abby, nearly dropping the broom. "What makes you think so?"

And now I turned the light on my dark voices, and told her everything, all my rituals from beginning to end, spewing them out like a bitter and humiliating confession. White horses and spilled salt and words that went cold on my tongue. The number of steps to the bedroom door and the long leap in the dark.

Abby listened gravely, glancing now and then at Miss Briggs, who sat insulated by the hot rushing air like a silent and skinny warrior.

"Well," she said at last. "Well, well. A devil. Yes, indeed."

She did not seem to understand what we wanted of her, so Mary Ellen explained.

"We came to you because we thought you could call him out."

"Ah," said Abby, as calmly as if we'd asked her the time of day. "Well, I don't know the words for it. Go get that little black book over by the telephone."

Mary Ellen brought the book and Abby thumbed through it slowly. At last her finger paused on a page.

"Here are the words for the exorcising of the devil."

She peered over her glasses, first at Mary Ellen and then at me. "A matter not to be taken lightly."

"No, of course not," I said, feeling myself in the presence of a great physician who would now perform a miraculous cure.

"If you're absolutely certain it's the devil, we ought to have the priest do this."

"I'd rather you did it, Abby."

Abby looked very pleased.

"Well then, you two stand behind that table."

Suddenly inspired, she went to the cupboard and took out the reliquary.

"There's nothing holier than the hucklebone of a saint."

She set it in the middle of the dressing table so that the mirror caught it from behind. Then she pushed Mary Ellen and me together, joining our hands on the relic as for a marriage, and laying the book open before her, she began to read in a loud voice.

I exorcise, thee, most vile spirit, the very embodiment of our enemy, the entire specter, the whole legion, in the name of Jesus Christ, to get out and flee from this creature of God. He himself commands thee, who has ordered thee cast down from the heights of heaven to the depths of the earth. He commands thee, He who commands the sea, the winds, and the tempests. Hear, therefore and fear, O Satan, enemy of the faith, foe to the human race, producer of death, thief of life, destroyer of justice, root of evils, kindler of vices, procurer of sorrows. Why dost thou stand and resist, when thou knowest that Christ the Lord will destroy thy strength?

Under my grasp, the hucklebone warmed. It had acquired for me a life of its own wholly different from its first life, just as it was Abby who read, and yet not Abby, but someone much older. Ancient, even. Not for Abby the beauty operator would the spirit of darkness depart, but Abby the magician's daughter, daughter of Eve, descendant of saint-seekers and wanderers of holy places.

Her voice was rolling like thunder as she turned the page:

Now therefore depart. Depart, thou seducer. He expels thee, from whose eye nothing is secret. He expels thee to whose power all things are subject. He excludes thee, who has prepared for thee and thy angels everlasting hell; out of whose mouth the sharp sword will go, He who shall come to judge the quick and the dead and the world by fire.

"Too hot! Too hot!" shouted a voice, and we all yelled, and I thought I saw the devil in the mirror and shouted to Abby, but then he shriveled into Miss Briggs making signs that she wanted to come out, forgetting, as the deaf do, that others can hear.

There was a snapping of hairpins as Abby pushed the dryer back and Miss Briggs emerged, as dazed as if she had awakened from a long sleep. Her hair lay against her scalp in crusted waves like cake frosting.

"What a funny color," observed Mary Ellen. "I believe your hair's darker than it was."

Miss Briggs sat down at the mirror and Abby took off the net and shook the pins loose. Nobody said a word for several minutes. Then Miss Briggs spoke up.

"It looks green," she whispered hoarsely. "Does it look green to you?"

Abby bent low for closer inspection, but you could have answered her just as well from across the room.

"It does have a sort of greenish cast. Sometimes a person can be allergic to the cream rinse."

"I never was before," said Miss Briggs, her face working.

Abby shook her head.

"I don't think a light rinse will cover it. You wouldn't want anything stronger than a rinse, would you?"

"Oh my, no. Just something to cover up the green."

"I could make it darker. Black, for example."

"Black!"

"It's better than green."

The silence prickled with voices. Why, Edith Briggs, what have you done to yourself? Would you believe it, running after the young men at *her* age?

Abby stuffed some change into my hand.

"Run downstairs and get two teas and some honey rolls."

Coming back, we met Miss Briggs talking to herself on the stairs with her hair hanging black around her face in big rollers, like spaniel ears. Abby was nowhere in sight.

When I got home, a palpable emptiness had invaded the house. Out of the dining room, with a rustling like blown curtains, stepped Oskar. He had been sitting alone in the falling light.

"They're all out looking for your grandmother," he said brokenly. "She's run away. Slipped out of the house while your ma was hanging up clothes."

"She couldn't have got very far," I said. "She has no money."

"No. But she's a strong woman."

She was found about five blocks from the house, headed, she believed, for the bus station. It had started to rain and the drops glistened on her big sealskin coat and her white hair. Mother hurried her upstairs and I heard the commotion—bath water running and heaters being turned on—that always arose when I came home from school with wet feet.

"She'll catch cold, you wait and see," said Oskar, sorrowfully.

She could not go outside now but lay in her bed, swathed in sweaters, while the radiators pounded in her room and the lights burned all night long. On the fourth day after her flight she decided to get up. She seemed to have gathered strength from her illness instead of losing it.

"I'll take her to market with me on Saturday," suggested my father. "Better to take her out than to have her run off again."

Market days were minor feast-days in our family. We bought honey and vegetables to last us for the week and sometimes such curiosities as acorn pipes and peacock feathers. Oskar and I would hold mock duels with our feathers all week till they broke.

It was unseasonably brisk for May. The egg-seller was warming her feet at a tiny stove and the honey-vendor had incarcerated himself in a little hut with a plastic window, behind which he waited as if for you to confess your sins. Grandmother walked among flats of pansies and beamed. For the first time that I could remember, she did not notice the cold.

She did not get up for church on Sunday, but lay whispering quietly in bed, unaware even of the presence of the doctor, whose attentions would have been a welcome diversion in her hardier days.

"For pneumonia at her age, there's not much hope. You should take her to the hospital all the same; the oxygen facilities there will prolong her life a little."

"I want to have no regrets," said my mother. "It's so dreadful to have regrets afterward."

My grandmother was put into a private room with nurses round the clock and a little cot near her bed for my mother, who told us how awful it would be to wake up at such a time and not know anybody.

But on Tuesday she was dead.

My mother came home from the hospital, her eyes ringed with blue. Neighbors brought in food, and casseroles—mostly chicken—began to accumulate in the kitchen. Suddenly plans for the funeral absorbed her with a thousand tedious details which ramified and consumed her grief. When Oskar stopped by our house that evening, she ran up to him, eager and awkward, like a little girl.

"I don't know how I'm going to manage. Oskar, if you'd only stay. You could sleep on the sofa."

"Wouldn't it be easier to put me in Grandmother's room? I'd be out of the way."

My mother looked flustered.

"Do you think you'd be *comfortable* in there?"

I knew from her voice that she thought nobody could ever be comfortable there now.

"Well, well, we'll see," said Oskar.

His valise in the middle of the floor announced his decision. Keeping a wary eye on the open door, my mother stripped the bed with a studied casualness. Never had I heard her move so quietly, as if she were afraid of awakening the air itself. Suddenly the door slammed and she let out a shriek of terror.

Oskar rushed in.

"Let me do it," he said.

And I heard him plumping the pillows and humming tenderly to himself, straightening the bed, it seemed, for the woman who had recently left it.

Darkness fell so gently that nobody remembered to turn the lights on. We did not sit down for supper, but picked at the casseroles spread out in the kitchen as for a church potluck. Oskar and my father, balancing paper plates on their knees, sat in the sun parlor, remembering death.

First Oskar remembered that the only extant photograph of his grandfather showed him in his coffin because Aunt Betty argued that a picture of him dead was better than no picture at all, and if you had the eyeballs touched in you could imagine him sitting in a first-class railway carriage.

Then my father remembered the funeral of a young girl he attended during a diphtheria epidemic, in which the mourners stood across the street and the coffin was tipped forward at the window by the girl's mother at a signal from the minister, who shouted his sermon from the front porch within hearing of both parties.

And then, in low voices, like children after the lights have been put down, they mused on the motions of the body after death. How hair and nails continue to grow and how the dead sit up in the furnace and their bones crack.

"You won't catch me being cremated," said Oskar. "When I'm down, I want to stay down."

At ten o'clock my father started the movement to bed. Last one up will be the first one dead—

I bit my tongue, remembering my newly won freedom, waited till the others had gone on ahead and then ascended the stairs. In my room I undressed quickly and started to jump into bed—

There is no one under the bed who will grab your feet.

I walked to the edge of the bed with slow and measured stride. Let the hands come if they dare. The body snatchers.

And then my mother's voice called out,

"Oskar, are you sure you won't be afraid in there?"

"Afraid?" His voice was filled with mild amazement. "Why should I be afraid? I loved the woman!"

His door closed, but I heard him moving around, and a light under the crack spilled faintly into the hall. Presently he opened the door.

The radiators were pounding. Mother had turned up the heat for Grandmother.

I got out of bed and stood in the doorway of my room and saw him, isolated in a little shell of light, as if I were looking at him through a mailing tube. He was sitting at the dressing table where Grandmother ate her breakfast, and he was writing calmly and steadily. I decided for no reason that he was writing a poem. On the back of a placemat, perhaps, or a menu, the surfaces which he preferred to write on above all else.

He did not see me. His back was turned and the light touched the thin places in his waistcoat with a soft shine. His habit of keeping his shoes on until the moment he stepped into bed gave him an air of expectancy at this hour; he would arise soon and go out for a visit, or perhaps someone was coming to visit him. Suddenly I believed that if he turned out his light, every light in the world would go out. Then there would be no more left of him than the hucklebone of a saint.

When the sun came up, his light disappeared. I was awakened by the sound of shoes dropping, and I dozed intermittently until I heard him shuffling quietly downstairs. There was a brief clatter in the kitchen and then the smell of coffee. I pulled on my clothes and went after him, trying to remember if my grandmother was already dead, if they had buried her yet, or if they would bury her today, but the only person I could find was Oskar. He poured me half a cup of coffee and filled the other half with milk.

"Do you want to take a little walk to the park?" he suggested. "Before anyone else gets up?"

We walked slowly past the teeter-totters and sat down in the swing, though the seats were wet with dew. My uncle glided back and forth, trying to keep his swing even with mine, swinging without a word, as though the morning had turned him young again and he knew no more what had happened to Grandmother than I did.

The Doctrine of the
Leather-Stocking Jesus

O N T H E day before Easter, in my father's garage, just before supper, I drew a chalk circle around Galen Malory, and said, "Now I am going to change you into a donkey."

"Don't," pleaded Galen.

He was five, three years younger than I, and the second youngest of eight children. His father had worked for forty years on the assembly line of the biggest furniture factory in Grand Rapids and was given, on retiring, a large dining-room table with two unmatching chairs. On holidays Mr. Malory sat at one end and Mrs. Malory sat at the other, and in between stood the children on either side, holding their plates to their mouths. The rest of the time, they ate on TV tables all over the house.

"Now you will turn all furry and grow terrible ears," I said, smoothing my skirt. "Heehaw."

"If I turn into a donkey," shouted Galen, "my mother won't ever let me come here again."

"Too late," I howled, rolling my eyes up into my head. "I don't know how to undo it."

Suddenly Mrs. Malory rang her cowbell, and all over the block children leaped over hedges and fences and fell out of trees.

"I have to go," said Galen. "See you."

As he ran out of the garage he bumped his big furry nose on the rake leaning against the door. He stopped, reached up and touched his floppy ears, and burst into tears.

Out of sight of God-fearing folk, we sat together on the compost pile where three garages met, and we wept together. I stared at Galen's ears, large as telephone receivers, and at his big hairy lips and his small hands browsing over all this in bewilderment.

His hands. His hands?

I looked again. I had not turned him into a donkey. I had only given him a donkey's head.

And I thought briefly and sorrowfully of all the false gifts I'd given him. The candy canes I hung on his mother's peonies, left there, I told him, by angels.

"Dear God," I bellowed, addressing the one power I did believe in, "please change Galen back."

"Somebody's coming," whispered Galen, terrified. "I think it's my father."

An old man in a brown overcoat and curled-up shoes was crossing the snow-patched field, poking the ground with a pointed stick. He was spearing bunches of dead leaves and tucking them into a white laundrybag.

"That's not your father," I said, "and he doesn't even see us."

But who could fail to see us? The old man skinned the leaves off his stick like shish kebab, put them in his pack, and sat down half a yard from us, nearly on top of the hole where a little green snake once stuck her tongue out at me. He pulled a sandwich out of his pocket and ate it slowly, and I saw he had dozens of pockets, all bulging, and sometimes the bulges twitched. We watched him wipe his hands on his coat, stand up, and turn toward us.

"Once a thing is created," said the old man, "it cannot be destroyed. You cannot, therefore, get rid of the donkey's head. You must give it to somebody else."

"Who?" asked Galen.

"Me," said the old man.

"I asked God to get rid of it," I said.

"I *am* God," said the old man. "See if you can change me into a donkey."

The smell of crushed apples and incense filled the garage when God stood in the center of the chalk circle and my voice weasled forth, small and nervous.

"Now I am going to change You into a donkey."

And because it was God and not Galen, I sang the rhyme that expert skip-ropers save for jumping fifty times without tripping:

> "Now we go round the sun,
> now we go round the stars.

75

.

Every Sunday afternoon:
one, two, three—"

Then I saw God stroking the tip of His velvet nose with one hand. His eyes, on either side of His long head, smiled at Galen's freckled face.

"After all, it is not so dreadful to be mistaken for an ass. Didn't Balaam's ass see My angel before his master did? Wasn't it the ass who sang in the stable the night My son was born? And what man has ever looked upon My face?"

"We have," said Galen.

"You looked upon my God-mask," said God. "Only the eyes are real."

He stepped out of the circle, opened His bag of leaves, and peeped inside.

"What are you going to do with all those leaves?" I asked him.

"I save them," said God. "I never throw anything away."

The leaves whirled around as if a cyclone carried them, as God pulled the drawstring tight.

And suddenly He was gone.

And now I smelled the reek of oil where my father parked his Buick each night, and an airplane rumbled overhead, and Galen was jumping the hedge into the Malorys' yard, and Etta called me for dinner.

And, conscious of some great loss which I did not understand, I went.

My mother and my sister Kirsten had already left for church to fix the flowers for tomorrow's service. Etta the babysitter and I ate macaroni and cheese at the kitchen table, out of the way of the apples waiting to be peeled, the yams and the onions, the cranberries and avocados, and the ham Etta had studded with cloves.

I wanted to tell Etta all that had happened, but when the words finally came, they were not the words I intended.

"Do you know what Reverend Peel's collar is made of?"

"Linen," said Etta.

"Indian scalps," I told her. "Do you know what chocolate is made of?"

"It comes from a tree," said Etta.

"It's dried blood," I said.

"Who told you that rubbish?" she demanded.

"Timothy Bean."

"A nine-year-old boy who would shave off his own eyebrows don't know nothing worth knowing," snorted Etta.

Etta gathered up our dishes and rinsed them in the sink.

"Can we go over and see the Malorys' new baby?" I asked.

When we arrived, Mrs. Malory and five of her daughters had already gone to church to make bread for the Easter breakfast. The Malory kitchen smelled of gingerbread, but nobody offered me any. It was so warm the windows were weeping steam. The corrugated legs of a chicken peeked out over the rim of a discreetly covered pot. Etta comfied herself in the Morris chair by the stove, mopping her face with her apron as she crocheted enormous snowflakes which would someday be a bedspread. Helen Malory, who was nineteen, plump, lightly mustached, and frizzy-haired, sat in the rocker nestling her baby brother in her arms. She was newly engaged to a mailman. Thank God! said my mother when she heard it. Helen's got so many towels and sheets in that hope chest down cellar, she can't even close it.

Today Helen had given Galen a whole roll of shelf paper and some crayons and now he and I were lying under the table, drawing. Because tomorrow was Easter, I drew the church: the carved angels that blossomed on the ends of the rafters, the processional banners on either side of the altar, the candles everywhere.

Galen drew Nuisance, the golden retriever who at that moment slept beside the warm stove. The dog's head would not come out right, nor the legs either, so he drew Nuisance wearing a bucket and walking behind a little hill.

Tenderly Helen tested the baby's bottle on her wrist and touched the nipple to its mouth. The baby squinted and pawed the air and milk sprayed down its cheeks. The lace gown it would wear tomorrow for its baptism at the eleven o'clock service shimmered in a box on the kitchen table. Etta was allowed to touch it before Helen put it safely away on top of the china cabinet.

"What are you giving him?" inquired Etta.

"Scalded calves' milk," said Helen.

"You could add a little honey. That won't hurt none. John the Baptist ate honey in the desert and he grew up strong as an ox." As Etta spoke, she peered at the baby knowingly over her glasses. "Is that a scratch on his nose?"

"He scratched himself in the night. His nails are so small I don't dare cut 'em," explained Helen.

"If it was mine," said Etta, "I'd bite 'em off.'Course I'd never bite anyone else's baby," she added quickly.

A white star gathered slowly at the end of Etta's crochet hook. Comfort and mercy dropped upon me in good smells that filled the kitchen. I was in heaven. I was lying in a giant cookie jar. Cuckoo, cuckoo, shouted the bird in the living-room clock. On its fifth cry, the grandfather clock in the hall started bonging away, nine times.

"Galen, take your thumb out of your mouth," said Helen.

Galen took it out and examined the yellow blister on the joint.

"I had a niece who sucked her thumb," observed Etta. "Her mother tried everything. When she got married, her husband said, 'I'll break her of it.' She finally quit when she lost her teeth."

"Better to suck your thumb than smoke," said Etta.

"Why?" I asked.

"It's wicked," said Helen.

"It'll stunt your growth," said Etta. "I had an uncle who smoked young. He never grew more'n three feet tall."

Deep in a shaggy dream, Nuisance growled and thumped his stubby tail.

"I think I'll latch the screen," said Helen, and she stood up fast. "Caleb Suarez told Penny if she wouldn't go out with him tonight, he'd come and break down the door. But I do love the fresh air."

"You want to go upstairs and see Penny's stuff?" whispered Galen.

"Sure," I whispered back.

I was more comfortable in the same room with Penny's stuff than with Penny. Penny was sixteen and religious, but like every other girl in the high school, including my sister Kirsten, she dreamed of Caleb and would dream of him long after she was married to someone else. Whenever she looked at her mother, she would burst into tears, and her mother would shout, "So sleep with him! Go ahead! But let me tell you, you can't get away from your upbringing. You'll feel guilty all your life. It's a sacred act, you don't just do it with any boy that comes along."

Caleb had black hair, all ducktailed and pompadoured, blue eyes, a handsome face, and a withered arm—the scar of infantile paralysis, my mother explained. His father was one-quarter American Indian and owned the Golden Cue Pool Parlor and came, when Caleb was

78

six, from Sioux City to find his relatives in Northville. There were no relatives, and as far as anyone could see, there was no wife.

Caleb spent his days at the fire department, reading and waiting for fires, and his nights drinking at the Paradise Bar.

"He's read all the books in the library; now he's starting the second time around," said Mr. Malory, shaking his head at such folly. "I will say one thing for him, though. I've never seen him drunk."

Galen turned on the light in the room Penny shared with Helen. Over a dressing table littered with bottles hung a big framed picture of Jesus, surrounded by photographs of brides clipped from the newspapers.

"That's Penny's," said Galen, pointing to the picture, though his voice was too loud for the room, as if he were shouting before a shrine. "We gotta go now."

"Did you tell anyone about God?" I asked.

"I wanted to, but I couldn't," said Galen.

"Me neither."

Down the hall, Helen was putting the baby to bed. Suddenly it cried furiously, and Galen and I hurried back to the kitchen. Seeing us, Nuisance lifted his head, and his rabies tags jingled like harness bells.

"Here, Nuisance," I called.

"His real name is Winthrop," said Galen. "He has a pedigree. If he had the rest of his tail, he'd be worth a lot of money."

Nuisance loped after me into the dark dining room, his nails clicking on the bare floor. China gleamed on the sideboard like the eyes of mice.

"Galen, get me a piece of chalk."

"If you change Nuisance into a donkey," said Galen weakly, "my mother will never let me play with you again. That's my dad's best hunting dog."

But he brought the chalk.

"Sit, Nuisance," I commanded.

Nuisance rolled over. I drew the circle around him and stepped back.

"Out of my way, Galen."

Galen did not need to be told twice. I fixed my eye on the golden shape of Nuisance, motionless, save for the stump of tail, which wagged.

"Now I am going to change you into a donkey," I whispered. And because it was Nuisance and not Galen, I sang to him:

"Nuisance go round the sun,
Nuisance go round the stars.
Every Sunday afternoon:
one, two, three—"

The sweetness of apples and incense hovered around us again. But nothing happened.

Then suddenly Nuisance jumped three feet into the air and, barking wildly, charged across the kitchen and crashed through the screen door. Etta shrieked and Helen came running.

"Is it Caleb?" she yelled.

"Nuisance broke down the door," shouted Etta. "You better lock him up good."

Galen burst into tears, and Helen sank to her knees beside him.

"There, there, honey lamb. No one's going to hurt you. Helen will lock the doors and windows." She held his head against her neck. "And I'll let you play with my Old Maid cards." Galen's shoulders stopped shaking. "And I'll even let you touch my new lampshade."

"Can I go down cellar and see your chest?" Galen said in a sodden voice.

Flicking the switch by the cellar door and taking each of us by the hand, Helen led us down the steps, dimly lit, past a clothesline sagging with diapers, to a big brassbound chest.

"Can I open it?" snuffled Galen.

"Go ahead," said Helen.

So Galen lifted the lid very slowly. It was like a thing from dreams, this box, big as a coffin, full of bedspreads and blankets and dishes. This is the way I would like to keep my whole past, I thought, folded away where I could take out last year's Christmas or my first birthday and play dress-up whenever I liked. Resting on top of a blue glass platter painted with turkeys, the lampshade waited. It needed a light to show clearly the man and woman walking in a garden painted on the front.

"I got it for seventy-five cents at a rummage sale," Helen announced proudly. "It's not paper, either. It's real satin, and all clean."

"Too bad it's purple," I said thoughtlessly, and then, seeing I'd hurt her, I added, "but I like the two people in the garden."

"What comes after the garden?" asked Galen, pointing to the edge of the picture.

"Nothing. Don't poke at it," said Helen.

And she herded us upstairs.

Etta had gotten control of herself and was crocheting as if nothing had happened, but her face looked like bleached flour. The lower half of the screen door was hanging out, torn in two—I touched it, awestruck. Helen went to the sink and started snapping the stems off the beans heaped on the drainboard.

"Etta," I said, and I felt my tongue thicken in my mouth, "Did you ever see God's face?"

"Nobody has ever seen God's face," said Etta. "Only His hinder parts."

Helen touched her buttocks absentmindedly.

"His what?" said Galen.

"His hinderparts," repeated Etta. "Nobody will ever see His face till the last day."

Etta knew the Bible better than any of us, but she didn't know I gave God the head of an ass.

"How do you know which day is the last day?" asked Galen.

"When all the signs have come to pass, that will be the last day," said Etta. "Oh, of course they won't all come at once. They'll be spread out over the centuries, for a thousand years in the Lord's sight are but as yesterday when they are past."

"Something's burning," exclaimed Helen. She peeked into the soup pot, pushed the chicken legs down, clapped on the lid like a jailer, and turned off the stove. Then she said to Etta, a little sadly, "All those things are mighty hard to understand—"

A crash outside cut her off. For an instant none of us moved.

"The raccoon is rummaging through the garbage pail again," Helen squeaked. "He comes pretty near every night."

We all exhaled.

"Go on about the signs," I urged Etta.

Etta smoothed a finished snowflake across the back of her hand.

"When my grandfather was a little boy, he saw the darkening of the sky. That's one of the signs. The cows came home and the chickens went to roost just like it was night. And stars fell out of the sky. People thought they would get burnt up, and some folks killed theirselves."

"Is this a ghost story?" asked Galen.

Etta scowled at him over the top of her glasses.

"I'm telling you what's in the Bible."

She opened her purse and pulled out a small book bound in white paper. "It's the new translation, and it only costs twenty-three cents. You could own three of 'em if you wanted to. And it's got pictures. See—"

"Who's that wild man?" demanded Galen.

"Where? Where?" cried Helen.

"There."

He pointed to the picture of a hairy man dressed in skins waving a big stick.

"That's John the Baptist," explained Etta. "But I believe this one is my favorite. It's from Revelations."

Over a crested wave, the red sun and the black moon bobbed like apples, and fish floated belly up among the spars of sunken ships.

"And every living soul in the sea shall die," said Etta.

"Fish don't have souls," said Helen.

Etta frowned.

"But that was the title of our lesson last week! What could it mean, then?"

"Don't fish have souls?" I asked, surprised.

"Of course not," answered Helen. "Only people go to heaven."

"What happens to the animals?" I hardly dared ask her.

"They turn back into earth."

"All of them?"

"All of them."

And my lovely spotted cat who loved nothing better than to nap by the stove in winter, would she too lie down in darkness? But I knew there was no point in asking about special cases if the rule applied to all. No doubt God didn't want puppies chewing up His golden slippers and peeing on His marble floors. I felt like crying. I could not imagine a world without animals. Even if I had none around me by day, I would need them at night. For whenever I could not sleep my mother would say, count sheep. I counted, one, two, three, four, and waited for the sheep to appear. But it was always buffalo that came to be counted, shaggy yet delicate, as if sketched on the walls of a cave. They floated out of the wall by my bed, crossed the dark without looking back at me, and passed silently into the mirror over my dressing table.

Suddenly I thought: if God doesn't mind wearing an ass's head, then why doesn't He let the whole animal into heaven?

"Not a one will get there, because they have no souls," said Helen.

"Do you think Nuisance will come back?" asked Galen.

Helen sighed.

"Dogs always come back."

"Tell some more signs," I said.

"In the last days," continued Etta, "God will send His star, just like He did when Christ was born. It will look like a big hand coming closer and closer. And then God will appear, not just to a few people in Sweden or Japan, but to everybody at once, like lightning."

Somebody tapped on the window over the sink, and a man's face lurched past, like a cracked moon.

"It's Caleb!" screeched Helen. "Don't let him in!"

We all rushed to close the kitchen door, but Helen rubbed the latch on the screen the wrong way, and in walked Caleb with his hands up, empty whiskey bottles on all his fingers.

"I've come to pick up Penny."

"Penny is at church," said Helen, her voice shaking.

"Church? Well, I'll wait for her."

"Suit yourself," sniffed Helen. "When my father comes home, you'll get it."

"Me and your old man are going hunting together next Sunday. Doves are thick this year."

"You shoot doves!" cried Etta. "Dreadful!"

Caleb shook the bottles off his fingers, one by one, and lined them up against the stove. Then he pulled off his sheepskin coat and threw it on the floor. Then he kicked off his boots. I could see skin peeking through his black socks like stars.

"Tell your dad to keep his bottles at home," said Caleb. "Tell him I saw ten empties running up Mulberry Street like a pack of dogs."

He drew up a kitchen stool and sat down.

"You can wait here till doomsday," snorted Helen. "No girl will look at a man who can't make a decent wage for himself."

Caleb smiled. He'd seen plenty of girls looking.

"I make a decent wage. I got my own place now too. A little cabin behind Mount Holly. No water except for a stream. No electricity. No cops." And then he added as if it had just occurred to him, "Why doesn't Penny want to go out with me?"

"Because you're no good," Helen said. "I ask you, what woman wants to sit up with a man on Mount Holly? A woman likes to be comfortable."

"Penny said that?" asked Caleb, surprised.

"Mother said it," admitted Helen.

I knew it was all over now with Mrs. Malory. Caleb's revenges were swift. When a Mercedes nosed his old Ford out of a parking place, Caleb came back to let all of the air out of the tires and stole the hubcaps. He sent snakes to those who spoke ill of him; Reverend Peel's wife received one in a teakettle, sent anonymously, which slithered out of the spout the first time she filled it with water.

"What do you do on Mount Holly?" I asked him.

"I watch for forest fires and make shoes."

"Shoes?" exclaimed Etta. "Who taught you how?"

"I taught me. When I've learned everything there is to know about leather, I'm going out to the West Coast to make me a fortune."

A thin wail brought Helen to her feet.

"The baby wants his bottle," she said brusquely, and hurried out.

"If you ever need a sitter," Caleb called after her, "I'm available."

Etta snorted, but Caleb paid no attention and turned instead to Galen.

"I've got a little present here for Penny."

And he bent down and began searching through the pockets of the coat he'd thrown on the floor. A couple of quarters spun out on the linoleum. A key ring with a medal on it plunked at his feet.

"What's that?" I asked.

"That's Jude, Saint of the Impossible," he answered, pocketing it and still searching.

"But you ain't Catholic, are you?" said Etta.

"No, I'm not Catholic. I got it from a buddy in the army."

"Do you believe in God?" persisted Etta.

Caleb shrugged. "When I was an altar boy in Sioux City, I wanted to be a preacher."

"You! A preacher!" shouted Etta, turning red. "The way you drink!"

"Christ drank," said Caleb quietly.

84

"And running around with women!"

"Christ ran around with a lot of women."

Etta was speechless. She wanted to walk out on him, but she could not take her eyes off what looked like a couple of leather bandages he was unrolling across his knees. Black leather, painted with flowers, the toes tooled with leaves, the cuffs studded with nails and, unmistakably, silver garters at the top.

"What beautiful boots," I told him.

"These are stockings," he corrected me.

"Leather stockings?" exclaimed Etta, astonished. "I never heard of leather stockings."

"Well, now you have," smiled Caleb.

He picked one up and stroked it like a cat, then laid it across the kitchen table. For the first time I noticed he used only one arm. I nudged Galen and whispered: see, one arm.

"How did you hurt your arm?" asked Galen.

I saw Etta close her eyes.

"Jumping down Niagara Falls when I was young."

Etta opened them again.

"How old are you?" I asked.

"Twenty-three."

This saddened me. Anybody over nineteen was, in my mind, old enough to be my grandmother. As Caleb was leaving, we heard Helen tiptoeing down the stairs. Waving to us, he called over his shoulder.

"I'm going to church, ladies. And if Penny is with anybody else except her mother and her sisters, I'll cut him in two."

The privet hedge was wet with dew. I hoped no slugs would drop on us as Etta pushed our way through.

My mother, barefoot, in her bathrobe, let us in.

"It's nearly midnight! Where have you been?" she hissed.

But instead of scolding Etta, she scolded me. "If you want to get up for the sunrise service," said Mother, "you'd better go to bed instantly. You and Kirsten are sleeping on cots in the kitchen. Your aunt and uncle are here. Etta, I made up the sofa bed for you. It's too late for a cab."

"My nightgown is in my room," I whispered.

"Never mind your nightgown," said my mother. "Uncle Oskar's asleep in there. You can sleep in your underpants. And if you smell the ham burning, wake me up. I've got it on low."

Kirsten was sleeping in the middle of the room with a pillowslip over her head, which she started wearing the night a bee crawled into her hair. Though I lay perfectly still, I could not fall asleep. The buffalo did not come to be counted, and the enamel pots hanging on the walls watched me like a dozen moons.

I heard my cat scratching faintly at the front door.

I got up and opened it, and somebody pulled me outside. But outside was inside; all around me, torches sputtered and popped, clothes smelt of pitch, and my spotted cat was no cat at all, but a girl in a pied gown who scampered away down the aisle that opened at my feet.

The church looked fuller than I'd ever seen it. In front of the altar, Reverend Peel, by the light of the acolyte's torch, was censing the people with a sausage in his left hand and a pot of smoking shoes in his right. He had wreathed his bald head in poppies, turned his vestments wrong side out, and thrown away his glasses.

"Kyrie eleison kyrie eleison"

shouted the choir from the balcony over my head. And the people shouted back,

Heehaw! Heehaw! Heehaw!

Helen was walking, with measured tread, down the center aisle, holding the baby wrapped in a rabbit skin. Diamonds blazed on her hair and on her eyelashes and on her white gown.

The King is coming, whispered Mother into my ear. The King is coming from a far country to bless the baby.

Everyone turned.

A donkey was walking down the aisle, its ears crowned with ivy, its legs sleek in black leather stockings, a scepter locked between enormous teeth. The moon sprang out of its left ear, the sun out of its right.

Riding before it on a black goat, Caleb, splendid in white buckskins, strewed grapes for the donkey's hooves to crush into wine. And loping along behind came Nuisance, ribboned with penny whistles piping by themselves.

Now a shout went up from every throat. And in that instant I knew this was no donkey, but a magician disguised as a donkey, and one far more powerful than I. Slowly the beast turned around, showing its handsome black stockings. It stepped up to the altar and laid aside the scepter. Helen held up the baby and it touched the holy water to eyes, lips, and ears.

When it finally spoke I knew the King had always been speaking, only I had not had the ears to hear. It did not ask Helen to abjure the devil and all his works, yet I knew it was not the devil. It did not promise salvation, yet I was sure it had come to save us.

"And some there be," said the donkey, speaking very quietly, "who have no memorial; who are perished, as though they had never been."

Over our heads, the carved rafters remembered their names: oak, ash, maple, and pine. They put out bark and leaves, and the angels carved there were no more. The scepter shrank to a hazel wand, but the beast did not notice.

"But these were merciful men," it continued, "whose righteousness has not been forgotten."

The glass in the windows blew away, sparkling like a million grains of sand. The pews rolled up into logs, grass grew between my toes, I could not see who stood beside me, and I could no longer remember my own name.

But the donkey's voice breathed over me like wind across a field: "Their seed shall remain forever. Their bodies are buried in peace, but their names live forevermore."

Then, not three feet away from me, Etta turned over on the sofa bed and sighed deeply.

The morning air raised gooseflesh all over me as I awakened, and I knew it would be cold on Steeple Hill when we gathered at the cemetery for the sunrise service.

Up on Steeple Hill, where all our people lay buried, a wind bowed the bare trees and sent the clouds scudding like foam as we waited for Reverend Peel to open the gates to the cemetery.

Most of the fathers, including mine, were home in bed.

Over the heads of the women and children, the gold cross swayed in the pastor's hands. The acolyte lifted the Easter banner high as a sail; its embroidered lamb sank and swelled, all heartbeat and pulse in the wind.

"Where is the sun?" I asked my mother.

"Behind the clouds."

"But how do you know, if you can't see it?"

"Because it's light outside."

Kirsten fiddled with the little silver cross she wore only on Sundays. She had a new pink coat, and I caught myself wondering how long before she'd outgrow it and I could have it.

His vestments blowing like laundry, Reverend Peel threw open the gates at last, and we marched in singing:

> "Holy, holy, holy! Lord God Almighty!
> Early in the morning our song shall rise to Thee!"

Are the dead surprised? Do they look at us, do they look at me? Does an old woman see her features in mine, does an old man see in Kirsten his young wife who died so long before he did? Do they sit in their graves as we sit in our pews, are we the service they wait for?

We walked two by two, singing bravely against the wind:

> "Though the darkness hide Thee"

How lovely it was there in the morning! Patches of snow gleamed in the shade of the headstones, but everywhere else the grass showed damp and green, though it had lain there the whole winter.

Theo's Girl

S H E   W O K E up suddenly, with the feeling that she had over-slept an exam. Someone was throwing stones at her window. She peered at the luminous dials of the clock; the hands said four. If I can get outside without turning on the lights, she thought, I won't wake anybody up.

But there was her mother, standing at the foot of the stairs.

"It's a mighty funny time to be going out with him," she observed. "Did you sleep in those clothes?"

"I just lay down in them. I didn't want to miss him."

"Sit down and eat. I got oatmeal made and everything. You want to ask Theo to come in?"

She couldn't get up earlier than her mother, try as she might. There was always that oatmeal waiting for you, no matter how quiet you were.

"I don't have time. He'll be late."

Her mother made a motion as if to throw it all in the sink, and Erica repented.

"Save it for me," she said. "Save it till we get back."

Theo was in the truck, drumming his fingers on the side-view mirror, and she squeezed in beside him. The back, empty now—its double doors clearly visible—resembled a sepulcher.

"Did you wake your mother?"

"Nope. She's still in bed."

"She didn't think it was funny? Like we were eloping?"

"No. She knows I wouldn't do a thing like that."

It sounded hollow, it hung in the air like a defeat. She should have been capable of it. As they drove out of the city and turned onto the superhighway, Theo stretched in his seat and leaned forward, resting his elbows on the wheel.

"Well, this is another job I'm going to lose. I've been late the last three times. It takes an hour to get to Detroit, another hour to bring the bagels back, and there's a line of people outside Sol's store by eight."

"You overslept."

"Clock didn't go off. The cat slept on the plunger."

They rumbled along quietly; she was falling asleep.

"Hey, wake up! Did I tell you about my new job?"

"Another job?"

"Yeah. At the undertaker's. There's a German family in town, wants me to make a death mask of the uncle."

"Aren't you studying for your exams at all?"

He gave a grand wave of his hand.

"I got all my sculpture projects in. All I have is French."

She leaned her head against the window, trying to keep awake. For days she had imagined the two of them, rolling softly, secretly, into the morning, and here she was, hardly able to realize it. The broad backs of the Ford factories glittered past, the river and the island flashed at them once and disappeared. When she opened her eyes, the heat of the city laid its weight on her, and the bakers were already running back and forth, red-faced, stuffing the last bags of bagels into the back of the truck.

"You goon! Some company you were!" laughed Theo.

But it was the trip home she loved best anyway, she decided, when the bagels filled the whole cab with a smell of onions and fresh dough. Theo reached behind and feeling the top of the bags, helped himself to a bagel, broke it, and handed her half. In silence they watched the sky lighten and the trees grow friendly again as the dark lumps of leaves opened to lacy green. The truck turned into her street; no one was stirring.

"I'll pick you up later if you want to come with me."

"Where?"

"To the undertaker's."

She lingered outside, one foot propped in the open door.

"If you want me to, I will. My Aunt Minnie's supposed to come today."

"She's still working to get you baptized, huh?"

"No."

"You know, if you let her do that to you, we're through."

"I know," said Erica.

"Well, what for, then?"

She had half a mind not to tell him, but she was no good at keeping secrets.

"She's taking us to Hannah's. Now can't you guess?"

"Say it."

"A wedding dress. Hannah's making it."

"Jesus!" He shook his head and smiled broadly. "You really mean it, don't you?"

She nodded seriously.

"I'll wear my *Croix de guerre* that I won in France."

"You've never been to France," said Erica.

Theo pulled a look of broad astonishment.

"Would I lie to you?"

"Mother says you've never been there or won any cross."

"My blue heron," said Theo, reaching over to stroke the hair which swung over her face when she put her head down. "If I can just get you out of here before you start listening to your mother."

Her mother was waiting in the doorway, holding her pink wrapper closed, watching them with that wistful smile she got sometimes.

"I kept it warm for you."

There were moments when Erica wanted to kiss her mother, like just then, but she would have felt funny doing it. Neither of them was very demonstrative. They went into the kitchen, and Erica got herself a dish and skimmed the crust off the oatmeal. Her mother beamed.

"You used to do that when you were a little girl."

She walked around the kitchen, talking, while her mother handed her things: orange juice, prunes, toast, always enough for a battalion. It was a mutual nervous mannerism, her mother handing her things, Erica taking them, putting them down here and there, talking while her mother beamed.

Far overhead, a cracked voice burst into "What a Friend We Have in Jesus."

"I forgot to tell you—Minnie came in last night," said her mother.

Every weekend she came, ostensibly to get her new Ford fixed. There seemed to be no Ford repairman in Detroit. On Sundays she drove back to attend church. When the semester ended, she would move into Kirsten's old room for long periods altogether. Kirsten rarely came home to visit since she'd married and moved to San Francisco.

"Minnie's taking us to Hannah's. But she's got to study."

"Study?"

"They're doing the new math in the fourth grade, and she says it's difficult. You got to learn it to teach it. She's got a new electric organ, she says. And a scalp vibrator."

Instead of a husband, said Theo somewhere in the back of her mind, and she shuddered. But Minnie had had husbands enough. Four. Two insurance men, a floor walker, and—the first one—an engineer. Erica could not imagine what it felt like to have run through so many. A different life with each one—did they fall away like so many winters? But when you repent of your sins, all that is changed and forgiven, said Minnie. Changed and forgiven. You are a new person in Christ. A new person.

And the husbands, thought Erica. Had they been baptized away, the hurts and losses drowned somewhere forever?

"I ate almost all the oatmeal," she said. "I'm sorry."

"Never mind. I can make some more."

Thump, thump. She picked up her orange juice and wandered into the living room. Her father peered up from the floor where he lay on his back, slowly raising his legs and letting them down again. Usually he was up before any of them. Once, on a dark winter morning, she had thought it was a burglar.

"We had a good time, Daddy."

"Eh?" His legs paused in mid-air, and he lifted his head. His gray hair snapped with electricity from the rug.

"I said, we had fun."

"Where were you?"

"Theo took me to pick up the bagels."

"To pick up what?" He had probably never seen a bagel, let alone eaten one. "He still got that old car of his?"

"No," said Erica. "It quit running. He abandoned it."

"Lord," said her father. He lowered his head and closed his eyes. Then he opened them again suddenly, as if something had bitten him.

"Minnie driving you to Hannah's?"

"Yes."

They never spoke much. It wasn't just the gap of generations, though; she didn't know what it was. Now that he was retired she felt she ought to speak to him more, but she didn't know what to say. All he could remember about Theo was that he had a broken car. Sometimes he asked if Theo had gotten the left headlight fixed yet, so it didn't shine into second-story windows when he drove at night.

The voice upstairs gave way to a chorus. Erica heard hymns jogging closer, as from a wayward procession; then they clicked into silence. She went into the dining room and Minnie looked up brightly. Her hair, newly tinted auburn, had an odd shiny look, as if it were cased in plastic.

"If I can just hear a good sermon," she observed, "it makes my day. It's such a blessing to me, this program. I'll be ready to go as soon as I find my teeth. I always throw them out, in the night. It's my bridge, with the two front ones on it."

And then, as she pierced her grapefruit into sections with the wrong end of her spoon: "Why do old people look so bad without them? I look at my kids in school; they lose them and they look cute."

In their identical pink wrappers, her mother and Minnie really did look like sisters, though Minnie was thinner and better preserved. Except she always *looks* preserved, thought Erica, and she felt herself getting depressed, as if some blight had touched her. She let her mother bring her a cup of coffee and tried to be cheerful.

"How old is Hannah now?" she asked.

Her mother considered.

"She must be in her eighties. Imagine, living all alone on that farm, with nothing but sewing to support herself!"

"She has a brother, though," remarked Minnie.

"Divorced."

"No, that was the other brother," Minnie corrected her. "Jonathan went into a bakery and made real good. And when he started, he drove the wagon for twenty dollars a month."

"She's got a half-sister who lives in town."

"She must have married well."

"No, she didn't. She taught piano all her life. I got a letter from her husband after she died, so I wouldn't send any more Christmas cards."

There was a long silence, during which they all avoided looking at one another. Then Minnie said slyly, humming under her breath,

"Is this your wedding dress Hannah is making?"

Erica had her mouth open to speak, but her mother got there first.

"It's just some white sewing. It could be a very nice graduation dress."

"I thought you told me it was satin."

"Lots of dresses are made out of satin these days."

"*White* satin?"

"Someday I could get married," said Erica in a small voice.

"*If* she decides to get married," added her mother. "There's lots of other things she could do. Paint, for example."

"You have to be terribly careful when you marry. They say you never know anyone till you're married to them," said Minnie. "Oh, I turned down some good ones, all right."

"Remember Irving Tubbs? I'd say you'd have made it best with him."

"Too late now," shrugged Minnie, without bitterness.

But already Erica had that sinking feeling again. They always seemed to be picking on her—not directly, of course, but in conversations she felt were performed for her benefit. My blue heron, I'm not your father, Theo would say. You don't want a father, you want a husband.

She thought of his little room over the laundromat; she had painted mermaids in the shower for him and had lettered his favorite epigram on a sign which he kept over his desk: ENERGY IS ETERNAL DELIGHT.

Sometimes they would lie down on the bed together and listen to the flute player in the coffeeshop next door one floor down, he wholly relaxed, she with one foot on the floor. For running.

That's how it is with you, he'd say angrily. Always one foot on the floor. Who do you think is going to come in, anyway? Your mother?

Did you lock the door? she'd whisper, agonized.

I locked the door, yes. Maybe your mother can go through locked doors?

"Immersion," Minnie was saying. "What have you got to lose? If the Bible says that you shall be saved through water and the spirit, why take the risk?"

"I'd feel a little odd about it," her mother answered. "If it's so good, why don't the Lutherans have it?"

Minnie shook her head. "Billy Graham preaches it. I'd arrange for a very private service."

"And you wouldn't tell anybody?"

"Not a soul."

Still her mother hesitated.

"Could I wear a bathing cap?"

"Did Christ wear a bathing cap?" asked Minnie severely.

Suddenly Erica felt ill. Why don't you say it, she thought angrily; he's an atheist, a confirmed atheist. It never bothered her until they talked about immersion, and then only in a sort of superstitious way because she felt she might be missing out on something—a heavenly reward she wasn't sure she deserved but might, by some fluke, get anyhow. It was that feeling of something left undone that bothered her most. Prudence—the seventh deadly virtue, Theo called it—and sometimes she felt that Theo was more religious than all of them put together. But art is not a religion, said Minnie. All the painting and sculpture in the world won't gain you the kingdom.

Erica had, somewhere, a paper napkin on which he had written, "Someday I will show you all the kingdoms of *my* world." They were sitting in the German restaurant downtown, which was always so full at noon that they could hardly hear one another.

What kingdoms? she asked him then.

My blue heron, he said. My little Eurydike.

And a few days later he took her to see his city, which he was starting to build on the empty lot behind the laundromat.

It was a city to be made entirely of junk, he told her. Already she could see it rising into shape as they walked between the walls made of washing machines, fire hydrants, clocks, mirrors, and fenders; between the towers made of wagons and marbles, bicycles and animal skulls, wired and cemented together: all the paraphernalia of human life.

And it shall be fifty cubits long to the east, Theo intoned, and fifty cubits to the west. And there shall be an hundred furnaces beneath the foundations and an hundred mirrors to catch the sun. And over the flagpole, a garbage can.

Where did you get the parking meter?

I took it from my room, said Theo. Didn't you see it in my room? I used to time my eggs by it, when I had a hotplate.

He sat down on a large bed, painted silver. He had stuck paper flowers in the springs. Around it the walls glittered with bedpans, coffeepots, and false teeth.

95

I have a hundred and five sets of false teeth, he declared solemnly. And a medallion of William Blake. You've got to learn how much is worth saving in this world.

Later they were crossing the alley behind Woolworth's on the way home from the nine o'clock show, and they both saw it: a pair of legs sticking out of a trash can.

Jesus! Somebody's fallen in!

The feet were hollow, the legs straight. Pushing aside broken boxes and excelsior, they set them upright.

Too bad it's only the bottom half, said Theo. Who'd throw out a thing like that?

Are you going to keep it? asked Erica.

Put it in the city, he answered. Grow beans on it, or roses. All my life I had to look at saints and flamingoes in my mother's garden. Nobody ever had a pair of legs like these. You take his feet.

As they emerged from the alley, a black car pulled up across the street.

Just keep walking, said Theo. And follow me.

He was humming happily to himself. He turned the corner with easy nonchalance and broke into a gallop. Erica, holding the feet, felt herself pelting after him.

You want to rest? he said at last.

They had stopped in front of the drugstore; a balding man in a pharmacist's white jacket was rolling up the awnings. The neon lights in the window winked out, leaving them in the blue mercurial haze of the street lamps. The streets were empty. They set the legs down on the pavement and seated themselves on the curb. In spite of the warm air of summer almost here, Erica felt a great weariness flood her like a chill. Theo reached over to touch her hair when she lowered her head.

Will you come and live in my city?

They arrived at Hannah's early in the afternoon. Hannah, on hearing the car, had come out to meet them and was standing by the pump in her long blue print dress. Behind her, the house, low-slung and weathered nearly black, crouched in the shadow of several freshly painted barns. She seemed to have been born ancient; Erica could not remember a time when her thin hair, tucked under the green eyeshade, was not already white.

"Afternoon," said Hannah, shyly.

As they stepped up to her, she kissed them one by one, a dry musty kiss on the cheek. The pincushion she wore at her lapel pricked Erica's face.

Hannah led the way through the kitchen. The low ceiling made Erica want to stoop. There was a wooden sink, deeply stained, and an enamel bucket with a chipped rim beside it. On a pedestal near the front door, a large Christmas cactus trailed its branches in all directions.

"A hundred years old," said Hannah proudly, "and it bloomed this year. I called the paper about it, but Mrs. Schultz had already called them about *her* cactus, and they wasn't interested in two of 'em."

"But you aren't a hundred years old," exclaimed Erica.

"It come with the house, I think. Oh, I could have had a sign out in front about the house, but Jonathan was never much on publicity."

They went into the living room for the fittings. Boxes of cards and buttons spilled over the wicker sofa onto a piano, which served as a shelf for photographs and birthday cards and was by this time nearly inaccessible; the keyboard looked permanently shut. On the sewing machine, with its faint traces of elegant scrolls, a cat lifted its head and blinked at them, then stretched itself back to sleep again.

For some reason the signs of faith were less depressing here than they might have been at home, thought Erica, forgiving Hannah the ceramic plaque, JESUS NEVER FAILS and the sign lettered in silver paint, GOD GRANT ME THE SERENITY TO ACCEPT THINGS I CANNOT CHANGE. On the walls, the sepia faces of an earlier generation looked out from absurd gilt frames. They were always stiff, her father told her, because the pictures were time-exposures and you had to wear a clamp on your neck inside the collar, that kept you from moving.

Suddenly she saw it, hanging on a coat-rack shining out over the faded coats brought in for mending and the shapeless dresses of old women.

"You want to try on the white sewing first?" asked Hannah, noticing her gaze. "It's just basted."

Her mother started to hum.

"I got some stuff for you to do, when you're done with that," she said. And Erica saw her studying the pictures on the wall, pausing before a confirmation certificate, lettered in German, showing in faded tints the parables and deeds of Christ. Stuck on the frame was a tiny star-shaped pin, from which several bars fell in ladder-fashion: five years, ten years, fifteen years.

"You never miss a day of church, do you, Hannah?" said her mother. "I'll bet nobody's got a record like you do."

"Raise your arms," said Hannah, and Erica felt the sudden cool weight of satin falling over her body. "Only one man had a better record than mine; he got the twenty-five-year bar, but the last year they had to bring him in on a stretcher."

She stood with her arms out while Hannah pinned and clucked to herself. Her hands were warm and light, almost like mice walking on her flesh, thought Erica. Minnie cleared a place for herself on the sofa and stretched out, running her eye over the dresses on the coat-rack.

"That's a handsome black one," she said. "Who's that for?"

"Me," said Hannah, "to be buried in. Thought I might as well get some wear out of it."

"Remember how Grandma had a dress she kept in her drawer to be buried in? White wool, it was."

"Fits pretty good," said Hannah. "Now, try on this overslip."

She shook it over Erica's head—light, vaporous stuff, embroidered with flowers. Full-skirted like a child's dress. Theo hated full skirts. Minnie bent forward to examine it.

"Imagine," she said, "a machine to put in all those flowers."

"How does it fit around the arms?"

Erica nodded.

"Good.'Course it'll take a little time—"

"No hurry," snapped her mother.

"—since I lost my ripper. I told Mrs. Mahoney to pick me up one somewhere."

"Mahoney?" mused Minnie. "Not Jack Mahoney?"

"He's dead now, just tipped over quick," said Hannah.

"Seems like all the people I went with are dead now," said Minnie softly.

Erica edged herself carefully out of the white dress, trying not to prick herself with pins. Her mother had already put on a lace one. Hannah and Minnie eyed her critically.

"Lace," observed Hannah. "Looks like you're going to a wedding."

98

"No wedding," said her mother. "Make it an inch shorter, don't you think, in the front? I haven't got a bosom like this—"

She pulled the front out like a tent.

" 'Course, skirts is shorter now," said Hannah reluctantly. "Even the choir wears 'em shorter.'Course a thing goes across the front so it don't show their knees. I could put some darts in the front."

"The lace is torn, too. Do you mend lace?"

"Lace isn't good except for weddings," said Hannah, shaking her head.

He wouldn't like the dress, thought Erica. She scowled at it, hanging on the coat-rack. He wouldn't like it because her mother had picked the design, not for his marriage, but for marriage in general. Somehow the dress looked like her mother. She did not know why.

Late in the afternoon, Theo appeared at her house, dressed in a black suit with a bag of tools at his side.

"You coming with me to the undertaker's?"

She had not told her mother about this job. They took her bicycle, she sitting on the seat, he pumping in front, his haunches striking her in the stomach as they pitched uphill, past the park.

"I can get off, if you want to walk."

"No, you're light enough."

When they arrived at the funeral parlor, they were both damp with effort. They reached for the knocker, but a man in a moth-gray suit had already opened the door. Over his shoulder, Erica saw the rooms, with their high ceilings and French doors, opening into infinity, multiplying like a house of mirrors. She remembered this house from her grandmother's funeral: the parlors where the dead awaited visitors and the carpets that flowed from one room to another, gathering up all human sounds. Was it in this large room that they had laid her out and Erica had cried, not for grief, but because her mother was crying?

The man led them over to a small group of people huddled together on a sofa at the other end of the room: two men and two women, all middle-aged, with pointed sallow faces. The women had covered their heads with black lace mantillas.

"This is the young student."

They rose and looked at him rather severely, then turned to Erica.

"My wife," said Theo. "She assists me."

The women removed their gloves and extended their hands to her. Then the taller of the two men inquired in an accent so pronounced that Erica wondered if it were real, "You have done this before? You know—"

"Of course," said Theo. "I have studied the trade in Germany."

"Well, then!"

They all looked immensely relieved. With a polite nod, the undertaker indicated that they might sit down and motioned Theo to follow him.

The body had been laid out, fully dressed, on a table and wheeled into a private room, empty save for a sink at one end. For a moment Erica caught her breath, but Theo gave her a look, and she said nothing. The undertaker lingered a bit.

"Won't take you very long, I suppose."

"No, not very long. You will excuse me—I prefer to do this work alone."

Blushing deeply, the other man muttered a little and bowed into the doorway.

"His face has already been shaved."

Pause.

"The family will be down in—say—half an hour?"

Theo nodded and waved him away. The door slammed, and his composure vanished.

"Open the tool case quick," he said. "Twenty minutes. Get out the plaster of Paris. Can you mix plaster of Paris?"

"I think so."

She rummaged through the little bag, pulled out a chisel and a towel, then a tin bowl and the bag of plaster, carefully averting her eyes from the body. Thinking only of what she must do with her hands, she carried everything to the sink, filled the bowl, turned on the water, and began to stir.

"Stir faster," cried Theo.

"You never really were in Germany, were you?"

"Christ, no. Give me the plaster—quick, before it dries."

Now she stepped forward and watched, fascinated, breathing very lightly to avoid the real or imagined smell of formaldehyde in the room. Theo had spread the towel over the body, tucking it in at the collar like a napkin. The face looked much like those she had seen upstairs; about thirty, she thought, maybe older. It neither grieved nor frightened her, this thing. Theo loaded his trowel and spread plaster over the chin and nose, then lathered it over the eyes and stood up straight.

"Now we wait for it to dry." He was looking cheerful again. "Who knows, maybe he'll come out looking like William Blake."

A kind of chill touched her at that moment.

"Where do you think he is—really?"

"Right here, all there is of him." Theo was washing his hands at the sink. "Your aunt been working on you again? Listen"—he looked very fierce—"if you let her baptize you, it's all over between us. Christ, you're not marrying me, you're marrying your mother!"

"They can hear you upstairs," she hissed.

"Listen," he said, in a gentler voice, pointing to the body. "*This* isn't anything to be afraid of. I've got to get you out of that house of old women."

"I think it's dry."

He tested the mask with his finger.

"Not yet. We'll wait a few more minutes."

They slid down on the floor, leaning against the wall in ominous silence. Presently Theo got up, bent over the body and took the edges of the mask in both hands.

"A little cool, but it's dry enough."

He tugged, carefully at first, then more roughly.

"Give me a hand," he said.

She stumbled to her feet and, suddenly nauseous, swallowed hard and touched the rough plaster edge over the ear.

"Push your fingers under it. You need leverage. Pull!"

"It's stuck!" she cried in terror. "Why is it stuck?"

"I think," said Theo, in an odd voice, "that I forgot to grease the face."

He had climbed up on the table by this time and was straddling the dead man's chest, clawing furiously at the mask.

"Chip it! Get the chisel! We'll chip it away!"

There was a muffled cry behind them, and turning, Erica saw that someone had opened the door. In the doorway stood the bereaved, their sallow faces livid with rage.

The tallest man made a leap for Theo but missed. Theo was already on the ground, and he plunged like a wild horse through the door. Erica followed him, running as if the dead man himself were after them.

They sat, shaking, in a cranny of rubber tires, at one end of Theo's city. The sun beat down on them, the hundred mirrors turned on their hooks and wires, and the springs, sleds, motors, rowboats, saws, clocks, flowerpots, and bedpans of humanity twirled past them. They sat in the shadow of a hundred furnaces.

"Best thing to do," said Theo at last, "is to forget the whole thing. A death mask, for Christ's sake!"

"If we were married and you died first, would you want to be buried?" she asked timidly, and realized, as she said it, that she was really asking something else.

"Ashes to ashes and dust to dust. No coffin for me. I want to go back to the earth."

A loneliness foamed up in her mouth when he said that. She had always assumed she would lie down with the rest of the family in one of the plots her father had bought years ago. Enough for the generations, he said. It wasn't a thing to take lightly. For when the trumpet sounded and everyone stood up in their graves, it was important, said her mother, to be among people you knew.

But by this time, lots of bodies must have scattered to dust.

The Lord knows his own, said her mother stoutly.

Erica saw them all very clearly, standing up in the graves and rubbing their eyes as after a long sleep, Hannah in the black dress she'd made for her funeral, her mother in the lace, Minnie, singing along with the heavenly host because she alone knew the words to the hymns, and herself in the white dress which would be her best dress forever.

"I took my French this morning," said Theo.

"You didn't tell me. How was it?"

"Awful. I flunked. I'm ready to pull out of this place." He touched her hair lightly. "And I want to take you with me. You got to trust me more, Erica. I'm not like your dad, but I'm all right."

"What are you going to do now?"

He shrugged.

"Go to some city, I guess. You can always find people in a city."

Suddenly restless, he jerked himself up. "It's hot here. You want to rent a boat and go the island for a swim?"

"I have to go home and get my suit."

"Jesus! Whoever swims near the island? Go in your underwear."

"A nice day," said the old man, sitting on a kitchen stool in front of the canoe shed. He looked past the open door toward the river, as if expecting someone to appear there. "Don't know why there aren't more folks out on the water."

The three of them went inside. Erica had yet to see a canoe in the canoe shed. Instead, it was full of nickelodeons, scrolled and flowered to resemble circus wagons, with the works decorously exposed. Behind little windows, the captive performers slept: drumsticks and cymbals, gears and piano rolls, perforated for the syntax of dead voices.

"Sign the book," said the old man, slipping behind a counter and handing Theo a pen. "You get number twenty-five. That really plays, Miss."

Erica was staring at the silver anatomy of a violin, spread open and joined to a hundreds of tiny threads and wheels, as if awaiting a surgeon. She had not noticed it the last time. On the glass was a neatly typed label: JUDGED THE EIGHTH GREATEST INVENTION IN THE WORLD. CHICAGO WORLD'S FAIR. 1933.

"It sounds just like a real violin. Listen."

The old man took a nickel from his pocket and dropped it into the back of the machine. From deep inside she heard a sputter and a whirr. Theo bent closer to look; then all at once they heard a nervous spidery response, ping! ping! Wheels spun, silver pistons scraped the strings. The whole effect was oddly touching, as if they were watching a fading performer's comeback from senility. When its shrill and complicated heart fell silent, they all three burst into applause.

"You don't know that tune, I bet," said the old man, pleased and shy. "Go out that door to the docks and take the first boat on the end. The paddles are inside."

The island looked small, the way places always looked to Erica when she had known them as a child and then revisited them as an adult. Rocks scratched against the bottom of the boat, and she climbed out, bunching her skirt in her arm. Theo lifted the prow, and together they pulled the boat over the thin strip of beach toward the trees.

"Come on," said Theo. "I'm going in."

He vanished into a bush. Erica waded along the edge of the water. The white skeleton of a crayfish surfaced as she dug her toes into the sand.

"Are you going swimming in your dress?"

She could not look at him.

"Somebody might come." But she knew there was nobody here but themselves.

"Good Christ," shouted the bush. "Since when is your own flesh a thing to be ashamed of?"

And when the voice spoke again, it was softer and more winning. "Here I am."

Drawn by its strangeness, she turned. There he stood, very white and thin-legged, and oddly exotic in his nakedness, like a unicorn.

"Well, I'm going into the water."

He plunged forward with studied casualness, but his whole body grimaced when the water touched his waist. Then he stopped and carefully splashed his ribs and arms, humming quietly to himself. In the sunlight, his back was as round and white as a loaf of dough. Dazzled by the brightness of things, gazing about him at the mainland some distance away, he seemed to have sprung from the dark flesh of the water itself. Suddenly a whistle bleated so close to them that Erica started.

"Are you coming in?"

He was looking at her, over his shoulder, which prickled into gooseflesh as she watched him.

The whistle hooted again, louder this time, and they both turned in alarm. A steamer, covered with tiers and tiers of children, was chugging toward them, under the green banner of the Huron Park Day Line. As the whole side of the boat broke into shouting and waving, she opened her mouth to speak, but Theo was already lumbering toward the woods, the water weighing him down like a heavy garment.

"Jesus!"

Now it was passing them, slowly and steadily, but she could see the children jumping up and down, and she could hear the way they called her, *Hey lady, hey lady!* not because they knew her but because they did not know her. She shaded her eyes and waved, like one who has been working and glances up to see something amazing, a unicorn in the bush, a caravan of pilgrims on the road, a shipload of souls, rollicking and rolling into the new world.

Sinner, Don't You Waste That Sunday

T H R O U G H the open door of the emergency room, she watched the nurse, a small black woman, caught like a moth in the light that dangled over her desk. Far down the dingy corridor, a man was singing:

> "We are poor little lambs that have lost our way.
> Baaa, baaa, baaa!"

Erica lay motionless on the stretcher, longing for the fresh air of the summer night, and as she listened, she saw the sheep wandering among the huge pipes in the boiler room—every basement had a boiler room—and a surge of pity for all lost creatures brought tears to her eyes. Who was the last person to lie on this stretcher? Cupboards hung open above the dirty towels heaped on the floor; bottles of rosy fluid peopled the table and the sink.

The singing stopped; the singer came into the room. He was a small man with dark graying hair and a pointed beard. In spite of his green gown and surgeon's cap, he still looked to Erica like a magician, and when he laid his hands across her swollen belly he seemed about to counter her fear with a runic spell.

"I should say the child weighs close to five pounds. If you woke up at three, you've probably lost about two cups of blood. Where's your husband?"

"Theo's parking the car."

"I'm sending you to the labor room. The nurse will tell him where you've gone."

A young woman in green carrying a clipboard pushed the stretcher, creaky as a baggage cart, to the elevator. The doors hushed themselves closed, trapping them both in the harsh light. Overhead, in hundreds of rooms, the sick were sleeping or tossing or crying out for pain in limbs that weren't there and nerves that were.

"When are you due?"

"Not for six weeks yet."

The girl said nothing more, but when the elevator lurched and stopped, she guided the stretcher through the doors, and turned into a small room, monastically white, furnished with a wall clock, a bed, and a nightstand which held a kidney basin. Handing Erica a shapeless white gown, she began flipping briskly through the papers on the clipboard.

"Let's see—you're Doctor Sloane's patient, and he doesn't believe in prepping." She reached into the top drawer of the nightstand, pulled out a razor and a syringe, and dropped them into her pocket.

"Age?"

"Twenty-one and a half."

Erica pulled off her dress, slipped the gown around herself and groped for the ties, but found none.

"Insurance?"

"I don't know. My father has some."

"Husband's occupation?"

Erica thought about that one, for there were any number of appropriate responses, all of them true. On Monday, Wednesday, and Friday, Theo cleans fossils for the owner of the Fur 'n Feather Pet Shop. On Tuesday and Thursday he sweeps out the cages for a nation of gerbils and myna birds. On Saturdays he makes frames at the New World Gallery for other people's paintings.

"Sculpt-or," she said, very clearly. "He's studying to be a sculptor."

"Student," murmured the nurse, writing it down.

Erica was just settling down among the sheets, when her stomach sucked into a hard knot. The intensity of the pain astonished her. She grabbed for the kidney basin, held it cool against her cheek, and threw up. How they anticipated everything here, she thought. Knowing that she would grope for such a pan, they curved it to fit her cheek. Her teeth chattered as if they had muscles of their own, and her whole body quaked.

Hands urged her body to turn; she felt a faint chill as the back of her gown fell open, but the needle came and went, sly as a thief. And suddenly there was no more pain, only a change of light, like a palpable anticipation of something not yet known.

> "Where is the way where light dwelleth? And as for
> darkness, where is the place thereof?
> Hath the rain a father? Or who hath begotten the
> drops of the dew?"

She repeated it like a charm; it was a gift from Theo. Asking the right questions, he said, was a way of keeping your balance. The first time she came to his place he was asking questions; he'd flunked his geology midterm and was making up an exam to send Professor Leech.

> "Out of whose womb came the ice? And the hoary
> frost of heaven, who hath engendered it?"

> Circle one: Mother Leech
> Mother Courage
> Jack Frost
> Admiral Byrd
> YAWEH

"What's YAWEH?" asked Erica.

"The secret name of the living God."

"If it's secret, how come you know it?"

"Because I am a student of the divine alphabet."

He had waved conspicuously but casually at the books that cluttered his desk. Erica had never seen so many library books in one place, except in the library. She fingered the biggest one, bound in disintegrating leather. *The All-Wise Doorkeeper, Exhibiting to all who enter, the Science of Things Above and Things Below.* A postcard fell out, typed with frightening accuracy:

You have three hundred and two books charged to your name. Please return or renew them before the end of the term. Books must be brought in to be renewed.

"There's a lovely sunset going on," said Theo, "for anyone sitting on the holy mountain."

Sitting on the fire escape, they could hear the bells of Saint Stanislaus and look across the vacant lot into the kitchen of Rumpus Mitchell's Hot Spot, and watch the greenhorn busboys sneaking out for a smoke among the garbage pails. Sometimes huge, fiery-haired Rumpus Mitchell would come out to meet his wife, who was always just arriving from California with Rumpus Mitchell's little boy at her side, and a little girl of uncertain origin still in her arms. The boy would lean against his father's great belly and the little girl would lie with her cheek on his shoulder while he sang,

"Sinner, don't you waste that Sunday.
Sinner, don't you waste that Sunday.
The people keep comin' and the train done gone."

When he was not outside he was inside, harassing the customers. To shy boys who brought their girls for coffee after a movie, he would say solemnly, "Who was that wild-looking chick I saw you with last night?" Erica had once seen him cut a man's necktie off with the breadknife, because he complained that the chili was too hot. The smell of chili flavored the whole block.

"I suppose you're hungry," said Theo.

The kitchen was cluttered with sketches of nudes and cats, and bishops turning themselves into flames. Erica was about to say yes, when she realized he was speaking to the battered orange cat that rubbed up against her legs.

"See if there's some milk in the icebox for Saint Orange Guy."

She opened the door and a slab of ice crashed from the freezer to the floor. On the bottom shelf, an ancient pork chop lay all alone, like a peculiar island.

"There's no milk."

"I wonder if Rumpus Mitchell will give me some fried liver on credit. It builds strong teeth and claws ten different ways."

He opened all the cupboards and peered inside. "All the dishes are dirty. I'll have to eat out."

"You could eat at our house. Mother made a meatloaf."

"No, thanks. I'll run out and get a pecan ring."

"A pecan ring! All you ever eat is pecan rings."

"So? If I get a fresh one, it'll last all day."

He walked her home. All over the city, spring touched the maples with lime-colored blossoms.

"I'll pick you up at nine for the free flicks."

"No, you won't. I have to finish reading *Rasselas* by Monday for my eighteenth-century class."

"So what's *Rasselas*?"

"A novel. Rasselas is the prince of Abyssinia."

"Jesus! What a name!"

"My dad thinks *your* name is funny."

"Oh, no," said Theo. "Mine's a lovely name. It means 'the son of silk and music, the immortal one, the heavenly music maker.'"

"You told me you couldn't carry a tune."

Theo shook his head.

"I used to play the flute in third grade during arithmetic. It was invisible. The teacher told my parents I was mad."

They stood on her doorstep, unwilling to leave each other. Out of the corner of her eye, Erica saw her father walking up and down the yard, tapping the pear trees that sprayed jets of white flowers into the air. Every fall the pears caught in the lawn mower; one year he had the trees injected to stop the harvest, and the next fall they bore twice as many. He hates anything that bears fruit, said her mother, who loved the trees and the overgrown forsythia and honeysuckle that ran wild in the backyard. Her father had taught chemistry and, according to legend, wrote caustic remarks on freshman bluebooks. At seventy-four, he walked slowly, like a mechanical toy about to run down.

"I'll call you," said Theo.

Her mother came out of the kitchen when she saw him go.

"You could have asked him for dinner. He doesn't have much moncy, and I don't think he eats very well."

"I did ask him," said Erica.

In the twilight of the dining room, crystal decanters and silver candlesticks gleamed along the sideboard. As a child Erica had laid out whole cities with them when they arrived, along with a grand piano, soon after the death of an aunt whom she had never seen. Most of her father's family she had never seen, and the little daguerreotypes didn't help much, for mildew had eaten away the image of a nose here and a shoulder there, and all the people in them were either children or brides.

"I've hidden the silver under the bookcase in the attic. You won't be afraid to stay alone for a week?"

"I'll be okay."

"Daddy would hate to miss the train trip and the banquet. He's the oldest living graduate of Grand River High School. And the valedictorian."

Her father glanced up from his ear of corn; kernels hung like tears on his cheeks.

"How many in your class?" asked Erica.

"Four," said her father, and sank behind the corn again.

"You can always sleep over at Mrs. Elderfield's place, like you did last year, if you're scared," said her mother.

It was always "Mrs. Elderfield's place," though Mr. Elderfield lived there, too. Mrs. Elderfield had a parakeet which she fed from her own lips at breakfast, holding grains of seed between her teeth. Mr. Elderfield had insomnia and wandered about the house at night in a red plaid bathrobe. At two in the morning he would go out and work on his driveway, which he was paving with bricks; the old widow who lived behind the Elderfield's told everyone he was digging a grave.

"I'll be okay alone."

Her mother lowered her voice.

"Don't forget to lock the door. We have all those Oriental rugs in the living room; someone could just roll them up as easy as pie. Then they could walk out with the color TV; I'm sure it would fit through the back window. I stuck your diamond ring over the curtain rod. They'll never think of looking there, though it would be a whole lot safer if you wore it."

"Oh, Mother, I can't. It looks like an engagement ring."

How quaint! Theo had told her when she wore it with him once to a movie. Engaged to your mother.

"It's a dinner ring. Everyone should have a dinner ring. I had mine made out of Grandma Schautz's diamond earrings."

A comfortable silence settled over the house as the taxi pulled away. Erica went to the kitchen and squeezed herself some orange juice, drummed on the piano for awhile and tried to play a few pieces from her mother's *College Favorites*, the only music in sight. Then, unable to postpone it any longer, she picked up her battered copy of *Rasselas* and curled herself in front of the dark television set to read.

I cannot forbear to flatter myself, that prudence and benevolence will make marriage happy. The general folly of mankind is the cause of general complaint. What can be expected but disappointment and repentance from a choice made in the immaturity of youth, in the ardor of desire, without judgment, without foresight, without inquiry after conformity of opinions, similarity of manners, rectitude of judgment, or purity of sentiment?

Someone had written in the margin: *up yours.* Erica quit reading the text and read the comments. There were two voices: that of the first owner, whose comments ran to obscenities, and that of the second owner, who had underlined all the speeches in red and crossed out the most offensive opinions of the first owner. Far away, the campus carillon chimed eight; she gave a guilty start and brought herself back to the text again.

Such is the common process of marriage. A youth and maiden, meeting by chance or brought together by artifice, exchange glances, reciprocate civilities, go home, and dream of one another. Having little to divert attention or diversify thought, they find themselves uneasy when they are apart and therefore conclude that they shall be happy. They marry, and discover what nothing but voluntary blindness before had concealed; they wear out life in altercations and charge nature with cruelty.

Her mind wandered; ten minutes on half a page! She thumbed the pages yet to come and felt panicked. By the time Theo called, she had read five more.

"I'm coming to pick you up for the nine o'clock show."

"I can't go," she moaned. "I have a hundred pages left."

"What have you been doing for the last two hours?"

"Reading."

A sigh breathed lightly through the receiver.

"We might as well have gone to the flicks. Do you want me to come over?"

She read on, listening for him, yet he did not come. At midnight, much disappointed, she locked the door, marched upstairs, kicked off her sandals and her skirt, and climbed into her mother's bed, because it was the only bed in the house with a soft decadent mattress and two purple eiderdowns. Finding her mother's book of Bible readings under the pillow, Erica pulled it out and lay there, listening to the dark till it blossomed into small cries.

Then she sat up and looked out of the window.

What green birds were these that pressed their masked faces against the pane? How cold we are! they pleaded, and fluttered their pale wings. Behind them, the pear blossoms were turning to snow. Kneeling on the bed, Erica unlocked the window.

I told you, said her mother's voice, not to let anyone in.

But suddenly the bedroom was filled with them, chirping feverishly, and already they looked larger than they had outside, and now they were flying up and down the stairs.

Out! shouted Erica, clapping her hands.

How had she failed to notice their fine claws and the tiny whips they wore under their wings? They poured past her and flew into the living room, caught the edges of the Oriental rugs in their beaks, rolled them up smartly, and carried them out of the window on their backs. The teapots and silver spoons under the bookcase in the attic began to rattle and hum, and the birds hustled them gaily out of the front door, which burst open at their coming. As the last birds passed her, bearing the color television set like a sedan chair between them, Erica latched the screen.

That inflamed them; the whips under their wings quivered; they rushed at the door with fierce faces, some hooded in black feathers like executioners, others masked in scarlet as for a dance. Hastily, she ran to the cellar, slammed the door, and turned the key. Crouched on the top step with her hands over ears, she heard—in spite of herself—vases overturning and drawers spilling to the floor.

Give some folks an inch and they'll take a mile, said her father's voice in her ear.

A pale green wing slipped under the door, groping. Erica backed down the stairs and clambered up on the big laundry tubs.

"Erica!"

A handful of pebbles hit the window by the bed. Pulling her skirt on, she ran downstairs to let him in. Drops of rain gleamed on his hair; his face was shining.

"So how are you, Ice-Maiden?"

She opened her mouth to protest and burst into tears.

"I thought you weren't coming."

"I had to arbitrate in a domestic quarrel. Rumpus Mitchell's wife blew up and wrecked his guitar. He cut her new poncho into shreds." Theo waited for her to stop crying, then he asked, "So what happened?"

"I had a bad dream."

"Why, didn't I promise to come over and guard you?"

She trudged upstairs with Theo behind her, rummaged through the big bureau in her mother's room, pulled out a torn sheet, and handed it to him.

"Some layout!" he observed. "Purple curtains, purple bed, purple rugs—it's a regular brothel!" He thumped the bed like a buyer. "Do you want to be tucked in?"

"Yes," she said.

He tucked the blankets into the mattress so tightly that Erica felt as if she were being swaddled; then he sat down on the edge of the bed.

"If you give me a couple of minutes, I can think of a story."

Once, when she had the flu, her father had come in to tell her a story. *Once there was a little girl who took a walk through a city where everything was falling asleep. The trees curled up their leaves and slept, the dogs dropped down on the sidewalk, and soon the little girl herself fell asleep.* He never came to tell another. That night she had dreamed curious dreams and forgotten them. In the morning, she felt she'd traveled all night in that land.

Now, years later, morning amazed her all over again as sunlight broke over Theo's back. She lifted her head; she could not remember where she was.

The doctor was greasing her stomach and smiling at her astonishment.

"We're going to hear from the unborn," he explained, holding—for her inspection—a microphone which was attached to an amplifier on the nightstand.

Under the sheet she thrashed her legs. Pain ran beside her, as inseparable from her as her shadow. Ah, now she was pulling ahead, but she knew it would cut through the forest and meet her at the next bend in the road.

"Give me something to make me stop hurting."

"You want a spinal injection after all? It will numb you from the chest down, and you won't be able to push the baby out. Fix your eyes on one point. No, not the clock; that only makes time go slower. Forget about time."

He pressed the microphone to her belly and adjusted the dials on the amplifier. Suddenly she heard a loud beating, a rhythmic thudding as from an invisible drummer, that seemed to fill the entire room and rose over the clatter of approaching wheels in the corridor.

"You see, he's still alive," said the doctor quietly.

She clawed her way onto the stretcher and felt herself borne down the hall with the slow majesty of a barge. Brass plaques on the walls passed her at eye level, with the discomforting solemnity of tombstones:

THE GIFT OF MR. AND MRS. LEANDER RICH
IN MEMORY OF HIS FATHER

IN MEMORY OF
DOCTOR JOSEPH O'BRIEN

A GIFT OF THE FAMILY OF
MR. AND MRS. JUDD CARUSO

The stretcher scraped against a small plastic box, quite empty, studded with lights and dials like an electronic reliquary. The legend passed her at eye level:

THIS INCUBATOR WAS DONATED—

Her feet touched bottom. The heavy metal doors swung open and she entered the cool air of the delivery room, where sunlight glanced off metal and glass.

"I'm giving you a shot in case I have to cut," said the doctor. "You won't feel it. If you watch in the mirror, you can see everything for yourself."

A plump woman in green scrubs lifted her onto the table, set her legs into stirrups, and covered her with sheets, as if arming her for a long journey. High in front of her shone the mirror, without reflection, like a child's dream of the sun. The nurse tipped it this way and that. Suddenly it caught someone: a man holding a syringe in one hand and an oxygen mask in the other. So strong a fear gripped Erica that she twisted her head back to see him.

"That's Doctor Wong, our anesthetist," said the nurse pleasantly. "We're required to have him here for emergencies."

"My glasses," called Erica. "Where are they?"

"Right here. I'll put them on your nose."

As the blur of equipment splintered into bewildering and exact detail, the masks and gowns warned her of sinister disguises. Nothing showed her an honest face. The anesthetist waited just out of sight; she could hear him padding about behind her.

"Push," urged the doctor. "One long push is worth ten short ones. Round your shoulders. Put your chin down."

Closing her eyes, she gathered her strength into a noose around the pain that had so long tormented her and pulled it tight. In the silence, the doctor's scissors snipped away at her flesh as if he were fashioning her from paper.

She gasped, and the nurse caught her head, and in that instant she felt something leave her and heard a faint watery cry.

He lay on her stomach, warm, wet, and crowned with blood. His skin flushed purple, white curds smeared the creases of his arms and legs, his eyes were cat-slits, his enormous mouth slobbered mucus.

"Into the world we come, pissing and crying," sang the doctor.

A wild joy filled her; her arms moved restlessly under the sheets, trying to find their way out, but already he was clamping and cutting the cord that joined her to this secret she had carried so long, and the nurse was lifting the child up and carrying him away.

"The bassinets used to be made of wood," she observed. "I like the clear plastic ones better. You can see through the sides." And then, after a pause, "I think he favors his dad."

Oh, when did he happen? In her mother's bed, among the Bible verses and the purple eiderdowns? Or that night they'd walked back from the library and stopped at the park to play in the sandbox—was he created to the comfortable creak of the merry-go-round, emptied of children at that hour, pushed slowly around by the wind? Or that Sunday morning, when they rode the river curled together in the ribbed body of a canoe, while the wild flags snapped and sank under them, but rose again in their wake—did he happen then? Far off, the bells of Saint Stanislaus rang the faithful to worship. It was eleven o'clock. Her mother and father, tired from the train-ride home, were nudging into their pew at Saint John's Lutheran and waiting for the opening prayer, which her mother knew by heart. Erica could not remember when she stopped saying her prayers. She used to pray before exams, and occasionally for advice, but she never expected an answer. During services, she ticked off the hymns and responses in her head, but came alive during the music and wondered what it would be like to meet God face to face. *All flesh is grass,* murmured the minister darkly. *The Lord have mercy on us.*

Let's get married next Sunday. In the middle of a forest, said Theo.

Erica rolled up her eyes.

You haven't got a job.

So? Behold the lilies of the field. They neither toil nor spin. We'll get jobs on a ship. We'll make love in every hotel in Europe. Then on to Asia. To Australia. There won't be a tree on this planet that doesn't know us, a stone we haven't baptized.

In the shallows before them, a school of carp lifted their finned backs above the water, splashing and leaping. Though the canoe caught them in its shadow, they heard and saw nothing but their own dance.

"Here's your son. Isn't he beautiful?" exclaimed the nurse. "He's a real peewee."

The head poking out of the swaddling blanket was that of a tiny old man.

"How much does he weigh?"

"Five pounds, two ounces. He's big for a preemie. I shouldn't think he'd need the incubator."

Through fear, through the craft of time and the cunning of pain she had almost lost him. The doctor, sewing her up like a turkey, had stopped singing. She saw herself leaving her inheritance for thieves to thrive on and setting out with the baby curled like a flower against her heart.

"Now we must get up," buzzed a voice in her ear. "Hang on to me. Don't look at the floor."

What time was it? She looked for the clock, but it was gone. The room was new; the sun stained everything in it with the rich glaze of twilight.

Clinging to the nurse, she allowed herself to be eased out of bed, and the new seams in her flesh stretched and seared her. The nurse was short, with thick glasses and a little sign on her breast that read *Miss Trout* like a nameplate on a desk. Over her shoulder, Erica saw a girl sitting up in bed, cradling a telephone receiver under her chin, and arranging a vast collection of cosmetic jars on the tray that swung from a stand across her bed.

"I'm little," said the nurse, setting Erica on a chair, "but I'm strong. You got some flowers while you were asleep."

She pointed: on the nightstand, between the bedpan and the kidney basin, stood a fat ceramic lamb rolling its eyes and spraying blue daisies from its head. The nurse picked up the card propped at the base, and read, "For that very special baby boy. Love, Mother."

"Did Ron tell you? He has blond lashes and eyebrows," cooed the girl in a singsong voice, pinching a clamp the size of a tooth extractor on her left eyelashes. "His nose is straightening out today. It looked so smashed. There was a little problem with his shoulder. It got stuck."

"Come," said the nurse. "I've made your bed."

How smooth and cool the sheets felt! When the nurse bustled out of the room, Erica felt herself becoming invisible, as if she were returning from the dead and had lost her foothold among the living. The girl's conversation seemed of immense importance, a token of the awful innocence of being alive.

"Today I had someone else's menu. It was lousy. Tomorrow I choose my own. Bring me a milkshake, love. A lemon one."

She hung up, and the eyelash curler clattered to the floor. Only when she climbed out of bed to pick it up, did Erica notice how tiny she was, no taller than a twelve-year-old child, with a round face and a large stomach that hung over her black bikini pajama bottoms. Erica moved her legs restlessly and the girl smiled.

"I'm Tina. You had the baby that came a month early, right?"

"Six weeks," corrected Erica.

"Six weeks! Well, better six weeks early than six weeks late. Two days over your due date, and you feel like you've been pregnant forever."

She worked her way into bed again and gave a curious little sigh.

"I got flowers with my first one, too. Yellow roses in a musical pram. We can't have any more; we only have two bedrooms in the trailer. Does the smell of nail polish bother you?"

"No," lied Erica. "I like it."

"Thank Heaven! My mother used to send my brother and me outside when she did her nails. In the winter it was awful, sitting out on the patio in our snowsuits."

Outside in the parking lot, doors slammed and voices drifted up through the window. Only later when the telephone woke her, did she discover that she'd slept through the visiting hours, and Theo had come, waited outside in the hall, and gone home again.

The line buzzed ominously. Her mother's voice sounded stretched and faint, as if she were speaking under water.

"How's the baby?"

"All right, I guess. He weighed five, two."

Her mother clucked.

"My first one came two months early. I even heard him cry. I suppose nowadays they could have saved him. For heaven's sake, don't forget to boil everything. I used to boil all your toys till they warped right up. What did the flowers look like?"

"Blue daisies."

"I told them roses. I've found a woman to help you. A trained nurse, so I'm pretty sure she's sterile." And then, a little hesitantly, "I've ordered you a sterilizer from Penney's. You didn't say anything about having one. You can't be too clean around a new baby. Minnie read in the paper that lots of people have parasites in their eyebrows. She's been washing hers every day. Just a minute. Daddy's coming."

"How is he?"

"About the same. He fell down again while I was going to the bathroom. One minute he's watching 'What's My Line?' and the next minute he's on the floor. I wasn't gone more than sixty seconds. 'Al,' I tell him, 'When you want to get out of your chair, call me,' but he always forgets. Sometimes I tie him in with the clothesline. Mrs. Elderfield offered to watch him while I'm in church. Last night I put the chest of drawers against his bed, and even then he got out. But when he tries to move everything, I hear him and I get up."

The phone went silent, except for the sound of scraping and breathing. Then a high voice whisked over the line.

"Hello."

"Hello, Daddy? How does it feel to have a new grandson?"

"What?"

"I said you have a new grandson."

"I can't hear you."

"A baby!" she shouted.

"What?"

She gripped the receiver in despair; she could hear him listening eagerly.

"I can't hear you." He sounded genuinely sad. "I'm so sorry. I just can't hear you."

"Erica, how are you feeling?" exclaimed her mother's voice.

"Better now."

"That's nice. Oh, isn't it wonderful how once you see the baby you forget all the pain?"

As Erica hung up, the nurse appeared with a tray of paper cups.

"This is your sleeping pill. If your stitches bother you, you may have a pain pill also."

What time was it?

Someone was drilling a hole in her sleep.

In the darkness she raised her head off the pillow. Far away, she heard the shrill cries of the babies, like tree-frogs on a summer night. Steps drew near and a policeman strolled past the doorway, his gun gleaming on his hip.

Now the cries mingled with the clatter of wheels. Tina stirred in the next bed. The nurses swept by, pushing trains of bassinets in front of them. The whole floor was a wailing corridor peopled with angels harvesting the newborn.

"Anapolous?" asked the young nurse in the doorway.

"Right here!" said Tina eagerly.

"Svenson?"

Erica raised her hand as if she were going to recite. The nurse snapped on the nightlight, rolled a bassinet against the bed, and lifted the baby into Erica's arms. His swaddling blanket held him stiff, like upholstery.

"Here's his bottle. You'll be feeding him glucose and water till your milk comes in. Don't worry if he spits up. You're trying to clear the mucus out of him."

Silence settled itself like a wing over the corridor. Erica took the bottle and touched it to the baby's lips, which sucked once, twice, and stopped. Behind the cat-slit eyelids, his pupils lay hidden, like agates at the mouth of a cave.

Who are you?

For his face was as blank as a fine plaster mask, without lines, without eyebrows, without eyelashes. Veins laid their complex waterways just under the skin on the top of his head, where the soft spot pulsed in the star-shaped absence of bone.

She pushed the bottle against his lips, but he slept on, his fine breath brushing her hand, and she pushed him up against her shoulder the way she had seen other women do. His head lopped forward and struck her collarbone, and he let out a quick cry, and Erica propped him in her arms and gave herself up to admiring him, till the nurse returned.

"How are you coming?"

"He fell asleep."

"You mustn't let him fall asleep. Snap his feet. Like this." As she unbound the swaddlings, his thin legs drew away like the amorphous flesh of a sea anemone. He cracked open his eyes and his arms stroked the air slowly and tenderly, as if he were feeling for the tides that had long since pulled out, trying to find the current that would take him home.

"I'll be back. See if you can get him to drink something."

"Five fingers, five toes. You beautiful little thing," sang Tina, and added, glancing at Erica, "My husband was born with six toes on his left foot. A club foot it was. So that's the first thing I asked: How many fingers? How many toes? Isn't it funny, all the boys I dated were six feet tall, and I married a guy five foot six with a club foot. It was a blind date. He came for me on his motorcycle."

Thunder muttered on the horizon. Outside, in hundreds of trees, squirrels were scurrying for shelter, foxes and moles were burrowing into their holes, and fawns were folding their matchstick legs under them. Erica shivered. Tina's voice was as warm as a lullaby.

"My little boy asks me, Where do the birds go when it rains? Why does Daddy have to go to work? All day long, it's why, why, why."

When the nurse returned, Erica put the baby in her outstretched hands and watched her tuck him back into the bassinet, where he lay like merchandise under the label above his head.

BABY SVENSON. FIVE POUNDS TWO.

And then, in scrolled letters below,

This is God's gift to you.

At nine the next morning, Theo peered into the room, holding a tumbler of wild honeysuckle.

"I tried to come earlier, but you were asleep. And last night the corridor was chained off. The nurse said it was feeding time. Jesus, I told her, what is this, a zoo?"

"Did you hand out candy hearts on Main Street?"

"I tried. Nobody cares anymore these days. I did all your crazy errands."

He sat down on the edge of the bed, searched his pockets, and brought forth a handful of cornflakes and a crumpled list. Erica recognized her own handwriting, but it looked strange to her, like a letter coming back because of an incomplete address.

"I got the undershirts, the diapers, the fruit juice, and the Borax. Also some loose catnip so Saint Orange Guy can roll his own mice. And I brought your watch."

As he slipped it on her wrist over the plastic bracelet which the hospital had put on her, she stared, fascinated, at the items and tasks she herself had numbered; they seemed steps in the irrelevant ritual of a dead faith. And the watch, ticking fast and small, so that not one hour should escape—what were those hours but a purpose laid upon things which run their course untouched by numbers and twenty-four-karat hands?

The hands tell her it is eleven o'clock. Her mother is nudging into her pew. *Sinner, don't you waste that Sunday!* Her father is home, tied to his chair, dozing in front of the television under the watchful eye of Mrs. Elderfield. In the hospital, visitors are arriving; the new mothers have put on their best nightgowns and their brightest robes, and leaning proudly on their husbands, they take their first painful, uncertain steps down the hall to the nursery, where they stand in front of the glass window and search the rows of bassinets for their child.

Here is the big blonde woman who wanted a boy and just had her sixth daughter, and the black girl who had a boy and walks about in a black satin robe that fits so tightly over her protruding stomach that she seems to be carrying him still, and when Erica meets them in front of the window, they chatter like old friends about the length of labor and whether the milk is coming in, and the husbands listen, bewildered both at the intimacy and the new concerns.

Theo presses his face to the glass.

"What if he grew wings?"

Erica looks at him, puzzled.

"What do you mean, wings?"

"He could be the first man on earth to be born with wings. We'd have to learn how to take care of them. We couldn't get them wet, or they'd lose their natural oils. Of course he couldn't fly right away, but we'd teach him to zip around. And we'd fold them up for him at night. 'Oh, Doctor Spock, my little boy has broken his wing, what should I do?' We'll walk him on a string, like a balloon."

And then he said, very seriously,

"When we're pushing eighty, he can fly us around on his back."

She nods, she is beginning to understand. Distance from the world has fallen across her, as if she breathed a different air and moved in a different space; the distance that separates those who sleep at night from those who are most alive during those hours and hear the first birds calling each other awake while the sky is still dark.

She sleeps with her feet curled against her belly, the way the child slept all the months she carried him, and she feels her body becoming his body, her face becoming open and small like his face. The folds in the sheet show her grotesque mouths, dwarfs playing invisible flutes, the running of foxes and the folded wings of birds flying through that forest she has not visited since her own childhood, lying awake in her crib, watching the shadows from the cars outside unleash wings and mouths and paws. And now, heavy-eyed with sleeplessness, she sees them keep watch around her bed; kindly rabbits and comfy bears, offering her their backs to ride as in the old days, before she learned to tell time.

By the end of the second day, her hearing has grown sharper and her sight keener. Before the babies are rolled out of the nursery, she feels their crying like an ache in her back. Every bird, every door cries with a child's cry, and she can pick out of all those sounds under the stars the one cry which she alone can answer. Outside, plans for the rape and salvation of the earth are going forward; factories rise up, and whole cities crumble away on command. Theo is performing all those tasks she laid on him before she realized that nothing is ever finished. With the baby resting against her shoulder, she is moving backward, away from the sun. Green birds turn their masked faces east and fly ahead of her, *this way! this way! Make way for the son of silk and music, the immortal one, the heavenly music maker.*

Behind the letters of the divine alphabet there is one face, just as behind every child's face lies the face of its father. How then, can she tell her loss to the young nurse who that evening wheels in only one bassinet and says, "Doctor Sloane has your little boy in the incubator so he can keep a close watch on his breathing. He'll be in to speak with you tonight."

Before the nurse can stop her, she is running down the corridor in her nightgown. The incubator has been moved into the nursery. How many times have she and Theo remarked with mild interest on that delicate machine, sitting empty in the corridor? Pressing her face against the window, she sees the child's belly heaving up and down inside. He lies in the intestines of an electronic bogeyman surrounded by more tubes than she can imagine uses for. One tube is taped to his nose, another to his arm, and they alone connect him to the cold air and harsh water of the new world. His belly flutters and grows still, heaves hard and grows still, like the body of a wounded bird.

So she arrives at last, and stands at the foot of the holy mountain, crying out to the Living God of Whom she has heard all her life.

"What's it all worth, Lord? Our bodies tear and our hearts break. You think anybody would choose this life if they could avoid it?"

But there in front of her the babies are wailing to be fed and even now, in millions of men and women all over the planet, blood is gathering and preparing once again to shape those frail bodies. The sun is crossing the sky and calling all green things to come forth, the pear trees drop their fruit, and the field sends up sumac and wild honeysuckle. All flesh is grass, cry the birds, and all flesh is beautiful. And breaking free from the flesh of their parents come the children, who have already forgiven them.

The Life of a Famous Man

H O L D I N G her suitcase very tightly, she stood on her toes and kissed Theo's ear and let him lift their son into her arms, then turned around and realized everyone else had already boarded long ago. A long long time ago. She turned and ran past the empty check-out desk and the unguarded passenger door, and skimmed across the dark airfield to the plane, which blinked and hummed, a huge comic animal, striped black down one side like a skunk's dream of flight. How cold, how dark the air was turning! She climbed up the steps, ducked her head, and hugging the child against her, stepped into the body of the plane, somewhere near its eyes. A stewardess, in a camel's-hair mini-dress, slammed the door behind her.

Inside, men and women were reading, adjusting their seats, squeezing their coats into the overhead racks. Erica worked her way down the aisle to a window seat over the wing. Nestling her suitcase under her, she buckled her safety belt, settled the sleeping child on her lap, and pressed her face to the pane of glass, very small, one vertebra among a hundred. Far away, behind a huge plate-glass window, the land people waved like observers at an aquarium.

The motor rumbled alive; there was a smell of shoepolish and gasoline as the plane turned, gathered its bulk, and headed for the broad road to heaven. Ahead of them, the airstrip was lit with tiny blue lights like cornflowers, bright on the bare field. Out of the corner of her eye Erica noticed a woman tenderly fluffing her hair. That, and the curve of Anatole's cheek against her shoulder, and the hands waving on the far side of the darkness crystallized and crushed her, as suddenly the earth seemed to split in two and she felt herself torn from him, tossed high, and snuffed out, over the fiery body of the plane that carried her. She did not know what sky or what field received them.

With a cry she awoke. Or was it the child who cried out? Beside her, Theo slept on. Groping for her glasses, she squinted at the clock. The hands pointed to seven; the plane left Albany at nine. The drive to the airport took two hours.

"Get up!" she shouted, jumping out of bed. A heap of books crashed to the floor. Already she saw her mother's disappointed face in the lobby of the air terminal in Detroit. And her father—would he be disappointed?

Theo opened one eye.

"The plane will be twenty minutes late," he said, as if he had learned this in his sleep.

Anatole was lying on his stomach in his crib, head up like a turtle, leaning on his elbows, babbling at the tulips she'd cut from the seed catalogues and pasted on his crib. His thin blonde hair lay in distinct lines across his scalp, like sea grass combed flat by the water. Not a hair out of place, she told Theo. Hair that only a mother could see, Theo told Erica.

She laid the child on the rug and wrestled him into his new blue overalls while the cold air mottled his skin, making all the veins prickle alive underneath. Would he take care of her when she got as old as her father? She could not imagine herself as old as her father, or this child coming to see her on her eightieth birthday—a finely carved edifice toppled by a stroke.

"My boon companion," said Theo, standing in the doorway, hands slouched over the waist of his levis, "Are you almost ready?"

Now she found herself once more at the passenger gate, kissing Theo's lean bristly cheek and taking Anatole from him, yet not exactly as she had dreamed it. In the dream—in all her dreams— she was younger and smaller and always alone, wearing the brown knee socks and red tam she still wore, and the green wool cape she'd lost long ago in the Cleveland bus station. And everything was dead quiet, as if someone had forgotten to turn on the sound.

"Am I crazy? I never came home for his birthday before. He has to have a stroke to get me home."

Theo pulled the sleeve of his army jacket out of Anatole's mouth.

"He's an old man. You don't need any other reason to go."

"Maybe," she whispered, "he won't even know who I am."

She found a seat next to a portly man with white hair who was gazing earnestly out of the window. The stewardess bobbed down the aisle with an armful of telephone books in kodak-yellow plastic covers.

"Would you like a magazine, sir?"

He closed his beat-up paperback copy of *How to Sell Yourself* but kept one finger at his place.

"What have you got?"

"We have *International Business, Business Week, International Travel—*"

Erica laughed. Cuddled on her lap, Anatole cracked open his eyes and sucked his thumb hard; there was egg, she noticed, on the cuff of his new sweater. The man looked at them both, puzzled.

"I don't believe I'll take any, thank you," he said, and opened his book to a chapter near the end: Failure Is Death.

"How old is he?" cooed the stewardess.

"A year and a half," said Erica. "Going home for his grandpa's eightieth birthday," she added, feeling it was expected of her, and as she said it, her father sounded oddly like a legend, not merely old, but ancient. He was fifty-seven when Erica was born, yet when she was five and going to school that first fall day, he walked so fast that she could not keep up with him. Every morning, after the news, her father turned up the radio in his room so that Erica could hear Uncle Buster, who at eight-thirty turned his magic eye on boys and girls, hurrying to dress for school all over America. *This morning it looks like the boys might win! I see a little girl in Oklahoma who isn't even out of bed. Now the girls are ahead: I see a boy in Illinois who can't even tie his shoes!* Erica did not like the magic eye and always got dressed in the closet.

Several years later she thought she heard that voice when she lifted her head to look at the clock during a spelling test. *I see a little girl in Detroit who can only spell half the words.* Who, thought Erica, could that be? She herself studied every afternoon for the sheer joy of it, walking over to the chemistry building and clutching her books as she climbed the dingy stairs to her father's office. Her father sat at a desk strewn with letters, calendars, photographs, and fossils, and she breathed in the strong clean smell from the adjoining lab. On the bookcase which reached nearly to the ceiling sat a white owl, the pet of a graduate student.

"Daddy, it's me."

He swiveled around and smiled.

"Well, you can sit here if you want to study. I was just going to finish up some work in the lab. What's this—a book on bees?"

He flipped through it.

"I'm earning the beekeeper's badge in Girl Scouts."

"But you've never kept any bees."

"I don't have to. I only have to give a report."

"I didn't know you were interested in bees."

She unloaded the rest of her books and pushed his papers aside.

"It's the first badge in the book. I want to earn them all, alphabetically."

As she read, munching on the sesame bars he kept for her in the top drawer, the radio in the lab buzzed the news. Russian troops were retreating across Poland. Outside, the maple leaves bobbed and washed and scattered the clear October sky. The sound of her father's footsteps was as comforting as a heartbeat. Now her mother said that he could not even stand up without a walker.

What was a walker?

When Erica called home, her mother would tie Daddy to the chair by the downstairs telephone, then run upstairs to the bedroom extension. He loved to listen in, though he never spoke much, and he couldn't hear well at all.

"How's Minnie?"

"Nutty as always. Ever since she moved in with us, she wants to take us to that health resort in Miami."

"That would be nice."

"But she wants to go by taxi, so we won't meet any hijackers. Did I tell you about her retirement dinner? The other teachers got together and gave her a bicycle."

They would chatter about Anatole and about Theo's new job as a monkey-nurse for the Zoology Department and how somebody had promised to come from a big gallery and look at his new piece— a galaxy of one hundred moons cut from old fenders—and hadn't shown up, and sometimes Erica could hear Daddy breathing, and then she remembered she wanted to talk about *him*. So after awhile her mother would say loudly,

"Nice talking to you, Erica. Good*bye*."

Adding a low whisper, "It's not a real goodbye. Don't hang up, Erica."

Then in a loud voice again, "Good*bye*. You can hang up now, Daddy."

Sometime he wouldn't hang up but would linger on, hoping to hear a little more, till Aunt Minnie came and helped him to his chair in front of the television.

The plane rolled forward, creaking softly, as if someone were pulling it by a string. Globes of light bubbled across Anatole's closed eyes. For an instant the machine hung back, then it gave a roar and charged. The child awoke with a cry and Erica lurched forward and grabbed him and clenched the armrest. All at once they were leaving the earth, it was angling away under them, and already the trees looked small and new. The man put away his book.

"Punkins down there," he observed, wagging his head at Anatole, who stopped crying and leaned toward the window to look. Below them lay the gold tarnish of the maples and the Monopoly board of human ambition, each field as straight as if plotted there at the beginning of time.

"Will you look at those trees!" he exclaimed.

"Where are you from?" asked Erica.

"I was born in Buffalo. Ever ride the old Wolverine that run from Buffalo to Detroit? I'm sorry to see 'em take that train off."

Sun burnished the hair that shone gold on his wrists, beyond the white cuffs. Had her father looked like this when he traveled to give lectures? She always gave him socks and handkerchiefs for his birthday, and he always left them in expensive hotels all over America. And when he came home at night—it was always night when he came home—she would stand by his suitcase, which lay open on his bed, and wait to plunder the silken pockets for the miniature bars of soap stamped with Statler or Ritz. Sometimes he remembered to ask the desk clerk for matchbooks, from which he removed the matches, for he did not smoke. She had, at the height of her collection, over a hundred matchcovers and forty bars of soap, which she could never bring herself to use, because having forty of them was more important than being clean.

And later he would bring out his slides, mostly of banquet tables where other chemistry teachers sat before water glasses and chrysanthemums. What was chemistry? She did not know. Not till she was sixteen did she understand that her father was well known to many who would never meet him. That summer, when her mother left for Coronna to see Grandfather through the last months of his life, Erica kept house for her father. She cooked great pots of squash and corn, tomatoes and Brussels sprouts, as she had seen her mother do, for he ate no meat, and she learned to shop at small expensive stores for the delicacies she knew would please him—pomegranates, mangos, and avocados. Evenings she sat at his desk in the sun parlor and typed his letters, mostly to young men in India and Japan who wrote—Honorable Professor!—begging the honor of studying with him. He stood behind her chair, leafing through the day's mail and dictating replies.

Sirs, I enclose two dollars. Please renew my subscription to the letters of Nostradamus.

She ended the sentence, but he did not bend over to sign.

"Erica, have you ever read the letters of Nostradamus?"

"Never heard of him," said Erica. "Who is he?"

"A prophet. Born in the sixteenth century. There's a medium in California who gets prophecies from him. Your mother doesn't believe a word, but maybe you'd like to read through them."

From the desk drawer he pulled out a package of mimeographed sheets and put them into her hand. She took them cautiously, as if they might burn her.

"What does he say will happen?"

"He predicts a great explosion on the West Coast, possibly an invasion."

After he had turned off the lights and she lay in bed waiting for sleep, she heard the loud whisperings of his prayers from the next room, and listening hard, she caught the sound of her own name.

A man's voice filled the cabin with the information that they were flying at thirty thousand feet. Yet it seemed to Erica that they were standing still, that nothing in this country was moving and nothing would ever change. Far across the shining pasture of clouds stood a farmhouse in an orchard, bleached white as in a negative, for all that showed her a dark face on earth gave her a light one here.

Fasten your seatbelts, please, flashed the sign over the aisle, and she tightened her grasp on Anatole, who was beginning to squirm on her lap.

"There will be a twenty-minute delay," crackled the pilot's voice, "due to fog in Buffalo."

But beyond the window, the sky dazzled her and hurt her eyes: a floor of clouds, inflated with light, stretched for miles in every direction.

"Why is it so nice up here and so bad down there?" asked a child's voice behind her.

"The weather," said a woman's voice, "is on *earth*."

Two hours later they plunged into a gray rain and touched down in Detroit.

From the passenger's entrance, she could see her mother standing behind the lobby railing. In her bulky plaid coat and babushka, she looked like a peasant woman around whom chic young girls eddied and vanished. How round her face looked under the pincurl bangs springing from under her scarf. Erica had worn scarves as a child, and curls—wetted every morning and spun around her mother's fingers. In the winter they always froze on the way to school and wept down the back of her dress all morning.

"I'm here!" called Erica.

"*Aw*," cooed her mother, reaching out to kiss Anatole's sweetly indifferent cheek, "what a little skeezix!"

They all three collided in an awkward embrace.

"You're too thin," said her mother, pulling back. "Have you been dieting again? Where's your suitcase?"

"I'm carrying it. This—here."

She pointed to the flightbag over her shoulder. Her mother shook her head, the way she'd shaken it the last time Erica came home, with her best taffeta dress mashed into her bookbag.

"How's Daddy?"

"Very quiet," said her mother. They walked toward the main exit across acres of light that filled the terminal—for all its traffic—with a luminous emptiness. "I don't believe he's said three words today. I had to call off the party. Thought it might be too much for him. But he wanted to come to the airport."

"You mean he's in the car?"

"With Minnie. I could hardly get her to drive out here, she's so afraid of getting polluted."

The cars glittered row upon row, like a vast audience waiting for the curtain to rise. What color was her father's Buick? Erica could not remember, though he had driven her in it often. He had even won a certificate from the Buick dealer for being the oldest man in the city to have driven nothing but Buicks for the last thirty years, ever since the day he stepped into his Plymouth, braked with the accelerator and flew clean through the garage, bringing down the clothesline in Mrs. Treblecock's yard. Like Superman, he walked away whole, attended by little puffs of smoke.

Suddenly she recognized his slouched tweed cap and ran to open the door.

"Daddy! It's me! Happy birthday!"

His face looked furrowed and brown as a walnut, and his white hair lay thicker than she had ever seen it. His eyebrows were so black that she drew back with a start. Always he had enjoyed the attentions of the barber, and the ritual of lathering and shaving each morning, of plucking stray hairs from his nose, and annointing his head with oil, so that Erica had never seen any part of him growing wild. She kissed his cheek, freckled and sunken, while Anatole bobbed up and down in her arms and reached for the planes that roared overhead.

"He looks pretty foxy, doesn't he?" said Aunt Minnie. She had put on her wig for this expedition, and Erica felt oddly touched. She knelt so that her son was eyeball to eyeball with her father.

"This is Grandpa. Can you say Grandpa?"

"Pa," said the child and stared at him.

"He knows you, Daddy. He carries your picture around at home."

Sitting in the backseat with Anatole on her lap, she touched his lips with her finger, but when she took it away, he went on making airplane noises and pushing his fist through the air over her father's head.

"Remember Sammy Elderfield?" her mother asked suddenly. "They have a new baby. You remember Sammy from second grade?"

"Not very well." She remembered a figure in a blue corduroy jacket but could not make out the face.

"They had a boy. It's a shame about his ears."

"What's wrong with his ears?"

"He has one of Mona's and one of Sammy's. Sammy always had lovely ears. Such awful things can happen—it's a wonder people have children at all."

Anatole leaned his chin on the back of the seat and his fist came to rest behind her father's collar.

"Can you say Minnie?" asked Erica.

"Minnie," said Anatole, peering into her purse and pulling out a blank check scribbled with wilting letters.

"Can you say A?"

He looked at his feet and said nothing.

"Oh, Mother, I taught him through G last night, and he's forgotten everything."

But when the car turned into the driveway, he said in a voice so small that Erica alone heard it:

"A."

At lunch, Erica could not take her eyes off her father, except to watch Anatole. Her father ate at one end of the table, silently spooning up puréed peas, and Anatole ate at the other end in Erica's old highchair, steering with a doughnut. Through the French doors she could see Aunt Minnie on the back porch in slacks and trenchcoat, rummaging among boxes and bags lined up on the sofa.

Her mother shook her head.

"She never sits down anymore, since she got so healthy. She eats only one meal a day, a protein drink."

"A what?"

"A protein drink. I'll make you one, if you like."

Aunt Minnie burst through the back door, clutching half a dozen vitamins to her bosom.

"I got some organic spinach at the market this morning, if anyone wants to try it."

"No thanks. You got to boil up half a pound to get a tablespoon."

"Where do you get all this stuff?" asked Erica.

"Why, there's a health-food salesman who comes around once a week," said her mother. "A young fellow. Isn't he nice, Al?"

The old man nodded, pushed aside the empty dish in front of him and reached for the stewed prunes.

"His hair was beautiful," remarked Minnie. "He told us about a program, guaranteed to help you or your money back. You eat one banana mashed in protein powder for breakfast, six lecithin tablets at each meal, and kelp flakes for dinner. En-Er-Gee Proy-To power. Very spluzy stuff, seven dollars a jar." She held up a small can, labeled with Atlas fully flexed, and glanced at Erica's father, who was leaning forward and straining his arms against the edge of the table. "Think that program is making him any better, Erica?"

"Daddy, stay with us for a while," pleaded her mother. "You haven't seen Erica for a year."

"I'll miss the kick-off," he said sadly.

Mother sighed.

"Erica, you take one arm. Al, push yourself up."

Though her mother helped to support him, Erica had never before raised such a dead weight. Yet it was he who taught her how to float when she was five, and his hands that let her lie on the surface of the water. *Now just let go. Don't kick.* Later, digging in the sand, she looked up and saw his belly rising far off like an island in the deep water where he floated for hours, as if he were napping in his own bed. Dragonflies paused there and flew on. In the water he took care never to disturb them; on land he took a net and caught them, and the butterflies too, so that Erica could study them and learn their names.

The three of them shuffled toward the television room. Not until she had to guide him did she realize how cluttered her mother's house was. Here in the living room stood Minnie's electric organ with its earphones dangling down the side, and there by the door were the two loveseats upholstered in horsehair, dreadful to the naked thigh. And her father so hated clutter: at the reception after Minnie's first wedding, he had gone round as happily busy as a child, folding up the chairs after each guest who went for a second drink of punch.

As she eased her father into his big leather chair she felt the muscles of her arms tremble. Orange light beamed through the plastic embers in the fireplace and played across her father's shoes. Her mother turned on the television and sat down beside him.

"We just had the downstairs painted, to the tune of a thousand dollars. Looks nice, doesn't it?"

In the old days, when Erica was at home, they didn't bother to repaint anything. When the blue paint started to chip off the bathroom floor, her mother said, "Paint me some flowers to cover it up." So Erica painted white roses around the gray patches on the stone tile, and went on to paint roses around the toilet seat as well. She'll paint on your coffin, warned Minnie. Mother had seen a flowered toilet seat—very posh, said Minnie—for twenty-four dollars, in one of the catalogues she read every evening. She had hundreds of catalogues heaped on the window ledge with her old piano music, back issues of *Fate*, *Time*, and the *National Geographic*, and some beautifully bound books on the history of witchcraft, which came after her dad started tearing out coupons for free offers. No salesman called—still, you have to watch him, Mother said.

"Who's playing?" asked Erica.

"I don't know," said her father.

It was the half-time of somebody's game. Out poured the band. Ta ra! A man in an absurd fur hat strutted out on the field, silver baton in hand, gold buttons gleaming. Behind him, the whole band was spelling out something very clever, but Erica couldn't read it. Then the camera cruelly discovered five men in business suits, puffing and twirling and squinting under their tasseled beanies.

"We bring you the a-*lum*-ni," shouted the announcer, as static from a storm far off blurred and flattened the five men into a single ruled line, zap zap into rainbow noodles, and back again. "Aren't they *won*-der-ful?"

Her father's head sank onto his chest and his eyes closed. Her mother jumped to her feet.

"Al!" she shouted. "Al!"

He stirred, opened his eyes, and gazed up at her.

"What's the matter?"

The fear slipped out of her face.

"Would you like a glass of cider?"

In the kitchen, her mother was calm again as she hauled the big jug out of the icebox.

"I always find him like that when I go to call him for lunch. He looks sort of pathetic, doesn't he? That's a clean glass on the sink."

What was dirty and what was clean? The telephone on the wall was gray with dust, and grease glazed the stovetop grill. Erica held her father's glass while her mother poured.

And as the glass filled up and chilled her hand, she saw herself at all the suppertimes of her childhood. *This is WXYZ. It is time for the six o'clock news. It is time for the weather. Fair and cloudy tomorrow. Small-craft warnings for Lake Michigan.* Her father's little portable sat beside his plate and opened like a clamshell, to show the crystals lying exquisitely under a sheet of clear amber, like the works of a watch.

Over her father's silence, Erica and her mother chattered, interrupting him for only the most urgent requests.

Pass the to-*ma*-toes, Al, pass the to-*ma*-toes.

Because if you didn't ask, he forgot to pass, and all the dishes stopped at his end of the table, and slowly, absent-mindedly, he finished them all. He would stare at guests as they helped themselves to seconds. There's plenty more in the kitchen, Mother would say. We have a whole bushel of tomatoes. And he would glance round with an innocent smile, and only then would they realize he had not been watching them at all. His eyes were bright as a rabbit's and very sharp, yet he did not see well, and that was why last Christmas he tripped over Anatole playing on the floor and nearly knocked him into the fire. It was a real fire that year.

When she was little, he carried a pince-nez for reading, and in the evening she watched it inch down the bridge of his nose toward the newspaper—plop!—and waited for him to jam it on again, and to fold up the newspaper and take out his pocket diary.

"Erica, what did I do yesterday?"

"It rained," said Erica, seating herself on the arm of his chair. "And it was hot."

Rain, he wrote, and frowned.

"Did I do anything else?"

"We went downtown to get your new reading glasses."

Looking down his nose he wrote *new glasses.* He was pleased that he did not need glasses for driving. The voice on the car radio that warmed the dark mornings when he drove her to school—how it sparkled with news of the cold weather as she climbed out of the car one morning, knew she was late, and slammed the door on her own coat. And as the car sped into traffic, how small her fists sounded, beating on the closed windows *stop! stop!* But her father was listening to the news and heard nothing; the light turned red and he stopped at the end of the block.

Later he sat on the edge of her bed with a wooden box on his lap and lifted out dark panes of glass, which came to life as he held them to the light for her. How could that be? To stay so dark in his hand and to show her nothing, yet when held to the light, to show her a table of ripe melons, dew gleaming on the rinds, and behind them, a bough covered with white blossoms.

What are they? she asked.

Autochrome plates. They'll never fade, he said proudly. He put the box back on the closet shelf. She never tried to take it down herself, for fear she would drop it. Fifteen years later, as she went upstairs, she knew she wouldn't drop it now.

She stood on a chair and peered at the clutter while her hands pushed aside old lampshades, broken cameras, small flowered hats, and velvet-lined boxes shaped to fit brooches long since lost; a gold pocket-watch without face or works, a pair of copperized baby shoes, an American flag, her father's bathing suit.

And here was the Adams hat he'd bought after ten years of listening to Lowell Thomas—or was it Drew Pearson? He bought it because it could be rolled up, would travel well, and would probably last forever. It came in a plastic tube and looked as shapeless as a gangster's fedora, and her mother hid it in the attic, though he sighed over it for a year.

Behind a half-crocheted blanket, she found the box, as heavy as if it held stones.

Downstairs, she found Anatole hugging the lid of a valentine candy-box between his knees and her father slumped down in his chair, and she could hear her mother stacking the plates in the kitchen.

"Daddy!"

She grabbed his shoulders and shook him, and he opened his eyes, and a huge sense of relief ran through her.

"See what I found, Daddy," she said.

And sitting down beside him, she pulled out a square of glass and held it up to the lamp over his chair. Between her thumb and forefinger stood a dark-haired woman in a salmon-colored Chinese robe turning her back on the camera, to show the dragon embroidered there. She was massive as a caryatid, yet she seemed to hang in empty space.

"Daddy, who is this?"

He squinted at the image in her hand and leaned his head so close to hers that she could hear his breathing, light as a cat's; could very nearly hear his heart.

"I don't know."

"Well, it's a lovely picture."

Suddenly Anatole scrambled up beside them.

"Look, sweetpea."

She pulled out another slide, held it up, and lo, ripe melons swelled deep yellow on a scarlet cloth under a bough covered with dogwood blossoms, and all were charged with the far-off presence of things in a dream.

"Daddy, do you remember when you showed me that one?"

He watched anxiously as she put the glass in its dark slot and it jammed against a postcard which pulled loose and fluttered to the floor. Erica bent and picked it up. Here was a house, but none that she knew. The upper window, diamond-paned, set in half-timbers, stood open to let out a queer procession of figures who seemed to be moving on a potter's wheel: the knight, the emperor, the priest, the angel, the fool; their course as fixed as the hands on the clock-face above them. She turned the card over but there was no message, only the name of the town: *Rothenburg ob der Tauber*.

"What year were you there, Daddy?"

"Twilight," he answered.

"But what year?"

"Why, the porter met us at the dock and put our suitcases on his bicycle and took us to the east gate. A wall runs around the city. There are two gates."

He paused, she reached for the card but he held it firmly.

"We stayed at the Golden Hirsch. They gave us the bridal suite. From the window you could see the orchards. Everything was in blossom."

Erica had not heard her father speak so much in years. Maybe never. Not to her, anyhow. And even now he seemed to be talking to himself. Anatole began to bounce the heart-lid on the floor, and her father's eyes followed it, up down, up down, like an aged hawk.

"Don't throw that," he whispered.

The child dropped it at once and turned stumbling out of the room.

Not until she went to bed that night did Erica remember she was leaving tomorrow morning. Anatole had pushed his head into her armpit and curled up against her, sucking his thumb. How warm he felt, and how little space he took in her bed! It was the same bed she'd slept in since her fourth birthday, and the familiar skyline of clutter still rose from the top of the bureau, loaded with books, drawings, unmatching knee socks, and velvet headbands. Overhead shone the paper stars that her father had bought; they glowed in the dark. The painter worked half a day with the dictionary propped on the stepladder, open to *constellations—northern hemisphere,* because her father wanted all the stars in their proper positions. Guests who used the room complained the stars kept them awake, but Erica loved them, and Anatole stared quiet and astonished at Orion, the Big Dipper, and the Little Bear, before he fell asleep.

Now the glue was turning brittle, and one by one the stars were falling. The first one fell on Theo's head the night he'd walked her home so late after a party that her mother said he might as well sleep in the spare room and go back in the morning. She heard him moving about—clothes dropping to the floor, change rolling under the bed, she closed her eyes, and all at once he was standing before her, as white and naked as a fish.

"I'm Adam," he'd said, and would have said more if they had not both heard the door to her parents' bedroom opening. He vanished with a bound into the closet, and Erica, going to shut her door, found her father, naked and hairy as an ape, eyes tightly shut, shuffling down the dark hall toward the bathroom. The next morning, at breakfast, she saw a tiny star tangled in Theo's hair like a sign of grace.

Anatole's breath moved her hair, and holding him close she opened her eyes wide. All those accidents, those chance meetings and matings! Extraordinary that out of each generation one had grown up and sent forth his seed, and that this seed should come forth at this time to create *this* child and no other. And then, that each child should survive the difficult journey from the immortal darkness of its beginnings to the cold weather of the world.

Someone was piling another eiderdown over them.

"Mother, what time is it?"

"It's two o'clock. I had to get up for Daddy. He wants to play the radio."

By the time she knew she was awake, her mother was gone. Muffled voices came from her parents' bedroom, and as she listened she felt the sheet under her turn warm and damp. Lifting Anatole in her arms she stumbled out of bed. The bathroom light cut a thin swath down the hall. Somebody had fed her, nursed her, and changed her for more nights than she could imagine. And when she was as old as her father, maybe somebody would again? She propped the sleeping child on the john, struggled to unfasten the back of his pajamas, and feeling something jab her side, she saw—for the first time—the lid to the valentine box he had smuggled into bed with him.

The sky was white; downstairs, Captain Kangaroo was singing to Anatole who had already escaped his bed. Erica jumped up and ran down the hall shouting,

"Get up! My plane leaves at ten o'clock."

Then she caught sight of her father, dressed in his best suit, perched on the edge of the bathtub, with a silver mirror in one hand and his electric razor in the other. zz-zzz-zz. Her mother was holding him up by his belt and reading the Sunday paper.

"Look, Al, Doctor Drake died. Now you'll be the oldest living alum. With him around you didn't have a chance. He was a hundred and two."

"Mother, my plane leaves—"

"Go downstairs. I got breakfast all ready."

Her father ate alone at the dining-room table—which was set as for a wedding breakfast with cut-glass goblets, brocade napkins, and the best silver—while the waffle iron steamed in the kitchen and her mother heated the maple syrup.

"Mother, I don't have time for breakfast."

"You can't take Anatole on the plane without breakfast. He can eat in front of the TV."

"He won't eat waffles, Mother. All he'll eat are hotdogs and bananas. Where's Minnie?"

"Upstairs, mixing her protein drink."

"I got to pack, Mother. Don't make anything for me."

Her mother pulled out the plug of the waffle iron.

"Erica, let me get you that little rocking chair of yours I saved for Anatole. I got lots of stuff saved for you."

"Oh, Mother, we don't need any more furniture."

"I got to get rid of things." Over the hiss of water gushing into the dishpan, her voice flowed without interruption. "Minnie brought all her furniture when she moved in, and it gets so we can hardly move. That's her umbrella on the front doorknob. I read in the papers how burglars break the glass and open it from the inside. So we'll hear them knock down the umbrella. The other night I was sure I heard a man in the attic. I went right up and turned the key in the lock, and I haven't opened it since."

Every leavetaking was like this, thought Erica, as she crammed her dirty underwear into the flightbag and rummaged the bedclothes for Anatole's undershirt. Her mother followed her from one task to the next.

"You want a glass of cider, Erica? You want to take that silver candelabrum back with you this time? I can put it in a big box and you can check it on the plane."

Standing in the front hall, ready to go: *how did I get all this stuff? I only brought one small bag.* There was a shoebox of sterling napkin rings, a shopping bag full of towels, and the candelabrum which didn't fit in any box. Her mother had powdered her face so fast that the powder lay in thick pools on her cheeks.

"Al, are you still eating? Hurry up, Erica has to catch a plane. Where's Minnie?"

A general sadness wrinkled across his face. How odd that she was traveling away from him instead of he from her! Always it was she who stood on the platform, holding her mother's hand—goodbye! goodbye! Bring me a present!—while steam frosted the windows, and porters pushed carts on great spoked wheels, loaded with mail bags and suitcases. Standing onstage at her high school graduation and waiting for her name to be called, she could see her father in the very back row of the auditorium, and she could see the clock on the wall, and now he was putting on his jacket and moving toward the door, hurrying to catch the taxi that would take him to the train. "Wait!" she wanted to shout. "Come back! It'll only be a moment longer! Four more names and it'll be my turn!"

And then, just before she heard her own name, she saw the door close behind him.

"I believe I'll stay here," he said, and his voice was frail as a husk.

Erica leaned over and kissed him, then picked up Anatole.

"Wave bye-bye."

But Anatole buried his face in her neck.

"He's forgotten. I'll come home again soon, Daddy." She realized as she said it that he hadn't asked. How dark his face looked, as if a light had burned out somewhere behind his eyes.

"Erica," said her mother, "Minnie is waiting in the car."

The backseat was suddenly full of packages.

"How do you think your dad looks?" asked Minnie, pulling on her gloves.

"About the way Mother described him."

"Thank heaven he eats okay. Anything you put on the table, it just goes. I left a quart of organic prune juice and a cheesecake on the table yesterday, and he finished them both."

"My God," said Erica.

"You know he never used to eat cheesecake."

The plane was not crowded, and she found a seat for Anatole by the window; they had a whole row to themselves. The smell of the vinyl upholstery made her feel queasy, and when she had fastened Anatole into his seat, she sat back and closed her eyes.

Opening them, she discovered she had come back to the little house in the orchard in the shining pasture that billowed like endless acres of fresh bread. Suddenly she wanted to walk there so much that indeed she was there, and here before her was a little station-house, weathered to pearl, and there sat her father on the platform, waiting for the train.

"I brought you a present," he said.

In the kindly light of this country he looked younger as he opened his briefcase and shook into her hands a dozen tiny bars of Ivory, Palmolive, and Camay, stamped with *El Camino Real*.

She tucked them carefully into her purse and sat down beside him, for there was no hint of a train. No bell sounded, no leaf stirred.

"When are you coming home?"

"I don't know. They've taken off the train," he said and shook his head sorrowfully. "Also the tracks."

"Oh Daddy, what a shame!"

"I'm real sorry they took off the train. There's no way to get back home."

"What station is this, Daddy? Where are we?"

He looked at her, puzzled.

"You mean you don't know either?"

Together they rose and looked up and down for a sign. There was none. But from the east, a little man on a bicycle was pedaling toward them.

"Your suitcase, sir?"

"Right here," said her father, and watched anxiously as he strapped it on the handlebars.

She raised her hand to shade her eyes; far off she could see the walls of the city.

"Have a good trip, Daddy."

"I do miss the weather," he said. "I mean, not having any." And then he added, "When are you coming back?"

But before she could answer him, the plane sank into darkness, and she saw the airport twinkling beyond the window. Anatole had fallen asleep with his head on her shoulder. Hoisting him up carefully, so as not to wake him, she grabbed the candelabrum and her flightbag and eased herself into the aisle.

As she walked to the passengers' entrance under the sullen sky, a fine rain was beginning to fall. She slipped her glasses into her purse, stepped through the last gate, and waited to be known.

"What," cried Theo, "is that thing in your hand?"

"A candleholder. My mother gave me some stuff. I checked the rest of it."

"Can't you go home just once without bringing something back? Wait right here."

He started to lift Anatole from her, but she shook her head, set the candelabrum at her feet and wrapped her arms around the sleeping child as if he were a life-preserver, kissing his eyes, his nose, his hair, till she realized the men at the ticket-desk were all staring at her. Nobody around her was kissing anyone; they were all scrambling for suitcases. How good he smelled! tasted!

"Look, sweetpea."

And she held him up to the window as their plane turned solemnly and glided down the runway, faster and faster, then tucked up its wheels and somewhere out of sight changed into a bird and broke through the heavy clouds into morning.

Salvage for Victory

"Salvage for Victory" is excerpted from Chapter 28 of *Things Invisible to See*, a novel set during World War II in Ann Arbor, Michigan. The scene is a conversation between a child and a woman who is taking care of him.

T H E   F I R S T   time Davy saw Ernestina, she was boiling water for tea and talking to Aunt Helen's teakettle. She was polite and persuasive. She told it the advantages of boiling; she told it about the other pots waiting to take its place. She put her hands on her hips and said, "Pot, what is your determination in this matter?" and the pot boiled.

Then she poured the water into Aunt Helen's flowered china teapot and added a tiny cheesecloth bag that did not smell like Lipton's and carried the tea out to the screened-in porch.

She sat down in the rocker and opened her purse, which was chock-full of khaki yarn. She was small, like his mother, but older, and her skin had the color of chestnuts fresh from the burr with the shine still on them, and her faded blue dress smelled clean and friendly as newly shelled peas. Davy drew his little stool near her chair and admired her. She did not appear to notice him, and he was much surprised when she said, "Loose tooth?"

He nodded—how did she know? He could wiggle that tooth without opening his mouth just by pushing his tongue against it.

"If you keep your tongue out of the hole, you'll get a gold tooth."

The blue jays screamed in the arborvitae; the cat lolled in the myrtle bed below, waiting for one false move. Davy breathed deeply the strong, sweet smell of the tea. Aunt Helen never let him sit near the teapot for fear he would knock it over and scald himself; and because she had forbidden him to touch it, he longed for nothing so much as a taste of tea from that pot. He gathered his courage and blurted out, "Can I have some tea?"

"Hoo! Not this tea," replied Ernestina. (Oh, would she let him try a different tea?) "This here is hog's hoof tea for my bad leg. You could bring me a cup. I don't know where your aunt keeps her cups."

Eager to please, he brought her a flowered cup from the cabinet that held Helen's best china. Ernestina thanked him gravely, as if he were a grown-up, and poured herself a cup and sipped it. Then she unlaced her shoes—black, with thick heels—and eased her feet out of them and wiggled her toes in their coarse black stockings. And what was that shining in her left shoe? A white stone?

"You have a stone in your shoe," said Davy, pointing it out to her, for she seemed not to notice.

Ernestina nodded. "The root doctor give me that when my leg got conjured. You can hold it if you want."

He picked up the stone and rubbed it between his fingers and thought he had never felt anything so old and gentle. And the rude doctor had put it into her shoe. That was a queer thing for a doctor to do.

"Can I keep it?"

"Nope. It come from the root doctor. My leg swole right up, and she dug under the doorstep and sure 'nough there was a conjure bag. Bones and hair and graveyard dirt."

Davy stole a glance at her afflicted leg, and she saw him; he could hide nothing from her.

"It do look fine, don't it?" she said. "The root doctor is a powerful healer."

Clackety clack, sang her needles, gathering the khaki yarn, arranging it to suit them. She held up for his inspection the front of a sweater for her oldest son. She had four sons in the army and one daughter away at college studying to be a teacher. Ernestina sent the money to keep her there, and it took a lot of money, she told him—it took practically all she earned. Her husband hadn't worked for a year; his liver was acting up. Before he got sick he wanted to join the Air Corps and be a pilot, but the Air Corps had no use for him, so he'd built a little plane of his own out of junk: broken radiators and old tires and rusty bedsprings, good scrap that the government wanted and would pay him for. He didn't tell anyone about the plane except a few kids in the neighborhood who came for rides. He had real pilot goggles for them to wear, just like his.

"Where do they go?" asked Davy.

"The Lord knows," said Ernestina. "The plane got no motor. But Henry keep a log book inside, with all the places."

Except for the lack of a motor, the plane was very well equipped, she assured him. She herself had never been inside to see where it went or how it got there because she was deathly afraid of flying. But she had seen the log and the names of the places. And she had seen the snapshots he took of the kids in those places. The backgrounds were always blurred, or common—a wall, a field—which convinced her that travel did nothing to improve your mind and folks might just as well stay home. Now *her* pictures were sharp; you could always tell what you were looking at. Did he want to see some of her pictures?

Davy was delighted.

She showed him four pictures of her sons in uniform and then a picture of her husband, radiant and cocky in goggles and pilot's cap, leaning out of a cockpit, and a creased snapshot of a young man posing under a palm tree. The young man was her brother who had died in Bataan and come back a week later and asked his girl friend for a pack of Lucky Strikes he'd left in a bureau drawer.

"He came back when he was dead?" exclaimed Davy.

"His ghost come back."

"Did you ever see a ghost?"

"Nope. But I hear 'em when the trees murmur. They 'round all the time, crowds of 'em, the bad with the bad, the good with the good. They don't mix theirselves up like living folks. And the good ones is always flying. If you feel the air from their bodies, you get well. Anything that bothers you won't bother you no more."

But though she had not seen spirits herself, she knew lots of folks who had. The good spirits looked like children, or birds. But they could be any shape they wanted to. Why, she knew the brother of a man whose wife took a drink from the spring at night and drank up the springkeeper. It took the shape of a snake, and that snake used to pop its head out of her mouth and whistle.

She set down her cup, and Davy crawled into her lap.

"Spirits is very fond of whistling," she remarked. "They do it to get your notice. If you ask 'em what in the Lord's name they want, they go away."

"If I ask one of the good spirits to bring me some springy shoes, will it bring them?"

And he showed her the picture in the magazine.

"Maybe," said Ernestina. "Maybe not."

A week later, when Aunt Helen and his mom were at the movies and Ernestina came over "to be in the house," as his mother put it, she woke him up and carried him to the window. The tops of the pear trees were blossoming hills of light.

"Full moon," said Ernestina. "You can wish on it. Show it what you want."

He opened the magazine to the page, and the moonlight fell on the springy shoes, a bargain at two dollars and ninety-nine cents.

"Is the moon watching us?" he asked. He loved the moon's dirty face.

Not the moon, Ernestina told him. The moon was just a lamp. But the Moon Regulator, who lit the moon every night—he would see the page. And he would send Davy those springy shoes. Not tomorrow or the next day perhaps. But he would send them. You never could tell which day he would choose.

She did not put Davy back to bed right away but let him stay up to see the stars. With the shortages, he was surprised to see so many.

"Hoo! They's just as many as they was 'fore the war," said Ernestina.

"Can they see us?"

"I 'spect they can. You never know who's watching."

From the solemnity of her voice, he knew these were grave matters, and he must not speak of them to anyone. And because no one had ever entrusted him with a secret before, he greatly looked forward to Ernestina's coming, and every morning he asked, "Is Ernestina coming today?" and mostly Aunt Helen would say no, but sometimes she would say yes, and then Ernestina would sip her tea (which she drank with ice in the hot weather) on the back porch, and he would sit in her lap, content to watch her hands twinkle the yarn off the needles. He had noticed that she never talked about herself to anyone but him. Only to him would she tell her troubles, and he listened politely, waiting for the squawk of blue jays, when he could turn the talk to his own liking.

"Tell about the jays taking sand to the devil."

"What's today?"

"Wednesday."

"They ain't doing it."

"Tell it anyway, please."

"Why you want to hear the same story over and over?"

"Tell about the jays."

"Well—they take a grain of sand a day till all the sand from the top of the earth is in Hell. They gonna ransom the folks down there."

The jays screeched.

"Tell about Hell," whispered Davy.

"Never been there."

"Tell about the coffins, then."

"Don't know why you want to hear the same story over and over."

"Tell."

"Well, there's Main Hell and there's West Hell. Bad folks' souls turn to rubber coffins and bounce through reg'lar Hell to West Hell. That's the hottest part."

She was fanning herself with a church program she'd found in her purse.

"I wish I were freezing, don't you, Ernestina?"

Ernestina shook her head no.

"I b'lieve I'd rather be too hot than too cold. I can't stand the cold."

And Davy, wanting to please her, said, "I can't stand it either," though just now he thought he would like it very much.

Mostly she talked about hot weather and cold weather, and how in the summer the iceman overcharged her, and how in the winter the furnace broke and once all her clothes froze solid in the washtub and Henry said, "I'll get 'em out," and he chopped them free with the ax.

"Chopped all my clothes to pieces," she said.

Davy never knew why, one night, after grieving over her ordinary disasters, she said, "The worst cold I ever heard of was Cold Friday. A man got froze at the gate of his house with his jug of whiskey at his lips."

Davy shivered.

"There was a funeral, and the heat departed out of the church, and the preacher and all the families froze solid. And the preacher's dog froze on the doorstep. They stayed that way all Friday. The root doctor was a little bit of a girl, and she froze right along with the rest of 'em. But the Lord saw fit to thaw her out. And soon everybody callin' her Cold Friday, on account she's the only one made it through."

Except for the regular creak of the rocker, the air held perfectly still, as if it were listening.

"Lord, Lord, she be a powerful woman!" said Ernestina. "Five times she died, five times she come back. She froze and come back, she drowned and come back, her house burnt up and she fell in the fire and come back, she got the sleepy sickness and was buried alive and come back, she choked on a bone and come back."

"I hear an owl," whispered Davy.

"Too early for owls," said Ernestina.

"I hear one."

"The owl is old-time folks. She won't hurt you. Oh, she was born the year the stars fell."

And he did not know if "she" meant the owl or Cold Friday.

FOUR LECTURES
ON WRITING

The Well-tempered Falsehood:
The Art of Storytelling

W H E N I was a child, my older sister and I had a game that we played on the long summer afternoons when supper was still hours away and we had nothing to do. We sat in our swings, too hot to move, until one of us started the game, and then we would forget the heat, the small yard with its mosquitoes, the impending supper, everything.

The game was simple. It required two people: the teller and the listener. The teller's task was to describe a place as vividly as possible. The object of the game was to convince the listener she was there. The teller had to carry on the description until the listener said, "Stop. I'm there."

I do not remember all the places we visited in the course of this game, but I do remember the very last time we played it. I was the teller and the place I wished to evoke was paradise. I did not know then that the damned are generally livelier than the saved, and that even Dante and Milton had wrestled with the problem of making virtue entertaining. Emboldened by ignorance, however, I began.

First of all, I filled paradise with the rich furniture of our own church. I put in the brass angels that held the candles and the stained glass windows in which old men read the Gospel to lions, dragons, and assorted penitent beasts. For how could I make paradise pleasant unless I made it comfortable? And how could I make it comfortable unless I made it familiar?

So I put in the hum of the electric fan behind the pulpit and the smell of peppermint that the head usher gave off instead of sweat. I fear it was a rather tedious description, and if I were to describe paradise for you today, it would be something like spring in San Francisco. And hell would be some bone-melting heat wave in New York City.

But however conventional the line I handed my sister, it was a lot more concrete than any account of the kingdom of God I'd heard in Sunday school, where heaven was treated the way my parents treated sex. Yes, it exists. Now don't ask any more questions.

At the height of my telling, something unforeseen happened. My sister burst into tears.

"Stop!" she cried. "I'm there!"

I looked at her in astonishment. I knew she cried at weddings and funerals. But to cry at a place pieced together out of our common experience and our common language, a place that would vanish the minute I stopped talking! That passed beyond the bounds of the game altogether. I knew I could never equal that performance, and we never played the game again.

The joy of being the teller stayed with me, however, and when people asked me, "What do you want to be when you grow up?" I answered, "I want to tell stories."

And the people to whom I said this always remarked, "Oh, you want to work on a newspaper, do you?"

I grew up thinking that if you wanted to tell stories, you had to go through the initiation rite of working on a newspaper, and that all writers had to do this before they could become proper story-tellers. When I was ten, I asked my mother, "How do I get a job on a newspaper?"

For it seemed sensible to get past this hurdle as quickly as possible.

"You apply for the job," said my mother. "But, of course, nobody will hire you without experience."

"But how can I get experience if I need experience to get a job?"

"You could start your own newspaper," said my mother. "You could start it this summer."

In the summer we lived in a small town on the edge of a lake. On the opposite side of the lake stood a gravel pit, which employed nearly all the men in the town. The quality of life in this town did not encourage reading. There was no library and no bookshop. There was not even a Christian Science reading room.

At night people went fishing or fighting. Lying on my stomach at two in the morning, my face pressed to the bedroom window screen, I watched the man across the street drag his wife by the hair down the front steps of his house while her lover fled out the back window.

I wondered how these people would like a neighborhood newspaper. I wondered if they would read it. I knew it would have to be free, as nobody in the whole town would be willing to buy it.

But there was an even bigger problem than finding readers. I hadn't the faintest idea how to gather news. Census takers were badly treated in these parts, and even the Jehovah's Witnesses had learned to leave us alone.

So I put the idea of a newspaper aside, until one night the lady next door dropped by for a visit. She was a large woman who made it her business to know everybody else's. She plunked herself down in our best chair to exchange gossip with my mother, who never had any but who knew how to listen to the great events of the day. What were these events? Ray Lomax was out casting for bass and hooked Mrs. Penny's baby through the ear lobe, John Snyder had been drunk five nights running, Tina O'Brien was pregnant by somebody else's husband, and so it went. These were the plain facts. Our neighbor's description of these facts would have done credit to the *New York Post*.

She paused long enough to smile at my sister and me. We were sitting at the dining-room table with our paper and crayons, and we smiled back.

"You like to draw?" she asked.

We nodded. She did not know that we had quit drawing the minute she opened her mouth and were transcribing every word she said. Here was news enough for ten newspapers! After she left, my mother censored what could be construed as libel, and my sister copied out the news in that anonymous schoolgirl hand she saved for thank-you notes and party invitations. We ran off our first edition on the wet face of a hectograph press, and we hung twenty-five copies of the *Stoney Lake News* in the living room to dry. The next day I went forth to deliver it.

We were an instant success. There is nothing people enjoy reading about so much as themselves. To see yourself in print—it gives you a kind of status. You are worthy of notice to someone besides your mother.

When I look over those newspapers now, I see the real news was not the events themselves but the people who lived them and who narrated these events to me. I heard some wild stories and I wrote them as I heard them. And I have all those people to blame for my prejudice toward fiction that is to be heard as well as read. In my mind, writing a story for a reader cannot be separated from telling a story to a listener.

I still marvel at how easy it is to tell a story, as opposed to writing a story. Collecting the news in that small town, I met people who could tell stories. Stories that left you breathless with suspense. Stories that made you laugh till your stomach hurt. All my storytellers had one thing in common, however. They would have balked at writing their own words down. They would have found writing stories very nearly impossible. But telling stories was for them as simple as conversation. Many years after the *Stoney Lake News* went the way of all pulp, I was reading *Tristam Shandy* and I came across a statement that brought back my brief career as a journalist. "Writing," says Laurence Sterne, "when properly managed, is but a different name for conversation." And I remembered, ironically, all those men and women who told me stories and who read little and wrote nothing.

The very old and the very young are natural storytellers. When you are very old, you narrate your past and it sounds like fiction. And when you are very young, you invent a past and it sounds like fact. Either way, all it takes is a listener to get you going.

I still envy the ease with which my son, at the age of seven, could tell a story. He would begin with no idea and no rough draft and no plan. But at ten minutes of eight, with bedtime in view, he would start spinning his tale. If he made it very exciting, he could prolong bedtime a whole hour. The problems of dialogue and character and plot did not trouble him. He moved swiftly from one crazy episode to the next. And listening to my son, I remembered the original goal of the storyteller: to entertain.

Let me say right now that there are many ways of entertaining a reader. Kafka and Joyce and Borges and Pynchon show us just how complex and diverse are the entertainments we choose. But I am dealing here with simpler fare, with the process of storytelling in a less subjective form. I am going to start with the first book that kept me up all night because I couldn't put it down. That book is *Household Tales of the Brothers Grimm.*

I still go back to folk tales and fairy tales when I want to lose myself for a few hours and come back to myself refreshed. Always the same thing happens. I read perhaps two stories and resolve to read no more, for I have to do the laundry or scrub the kitchen floor. But I happen to glance at the opening sentence of a third story, and the pull is irresistible:

One day an old man and his wife were sitting in front of their poor hut, resting from their work, when a magnificent carriage drawn by four black stallions came driving up and a richly dressed gentleman stepped out.[1]

And now I can't put the story down until I know who the stranger is and why he has come.

Or take another story, which opens not with an unfamiliar guest but with a familiar grief:

It is a long time ago now, as much as two thousand years maybe, that there was a rich man and he had a wife and she was beautiful and good, and they loved each other very much but they had no children even though they wanted some so much, the wife prayed and prayed for one both day and night, and still they did not get one.[2]

And with that sentence I am hooked. I know the story will tell me how she did get one. Fairy tales generally start at the point when somebody's fortunes change, for better or worse. And I know that the woman in this story will not get her child the way most of humanity gets children. Fairy tales deal with exceptional events rather than ordinary ones. And as I read on, I am not disappointed:

In front of their house was a yard and in the yard stood a juniper tree. Once, in wintertime, the woman stood under the tree and peeled herself an apple, and as she was peeling the apple she cut her finger and the blood fell onto the snow. "Ah," said the woman and sighed a deep sigh, and she looked at the blood before her and her heart ached. "If I only had a child as red as blood and as white as snow." And as she said it, it made her feel very happy, as if it was really going to happen. And so she went into the house, and a month went by, the snow was gone; and two months, and everything was green; and three months, and the flowers came up out of the ground; and four months, and all the trees in the woods sprouted and the green branches grew dense and tangled with one another and the little birds sang so that the woods echoed, and the blossoms fell from the trees; and so five months were gone, and she stood under the juniper tree and it smelled so sweet her heart leaped and she fell on her knees and was beside herself with happiness; and six months had gone by, the fruit grew round and heavy and she was very still, and seven months, and she snatched the juniper berries and ate them so greedily she became sad and ill; and so the eighth month went by, and she called her husband and cried and said, "When I die, bury me under the juniper." And she was comforted and felt happy, but when the nine months

157

were gone, she had a child as white as snow and as red as blood and when she saw it she was so happy that she died.

And so her husband buried her under the juniper tree and began to cry and cried very bitterly; and then for a time he cried more gently and when he had cried some more he stopped crying and more time passed and he took himself another wife.[3]

Now consider for a moment what a miracle of economy you have just read. In two paragraphs a year passes but is not glossed over carelessly, one character dies, another is born, and a third remarries, and the storyteller shows all this so simply yet so concretely that I think nobody could wish for more details. There is something about the process of telling a story that forces you to come right to the point. When you are writing a story, how often does the simple action seem insufficient? And how often do you feel you must analyze or explain it? But when you are telling a story, your first impulse is to create your characters through what they do. You, the author, become the invisible medium through which they live.

I am, to be sure, dealing here with a kind of fiction that emphasizes a linear plot. I know there are many kinds of storytellers and many writers who write as if they were talking to us. I have already mentioned Laurence Sterne. I could also have mentioned Mark Twain.

But the great books of these men were written, first of all, to be read, not just heard, and although they can be read aloud magnificently, a clear understanding of their work comes only when you have the books in your hand and can reread some chapters and compare others, and follow themes and characters over many pages. These are the pleasures of long fiction. When I speak of storytelling here, I am talking about the story as it is told to a listener.

I think it is good for writers to have that experience of telling a story. In my writing classes at Vassar, I sometimes try an exercise designed to give students that experience. We make up a story together. It's rather like making a crazy quilt. You tell your episode, and when your imagination fails, you pass it on to your neighbor, who picks up where you left off. I start by giving my students a list of ten or fifteen characters, which they may use if they are desperate or which they may abandon if they wish to make up their own. The list might go something like this: man, daughter, son, grandfather, magician, devil, car salesman, banker, angel, thief. I start the story by introducing a character whose strong passion for someone or something is likely to get him into difficulty. I say, "Once upon a time there was a woman who loved cars more than anything else in the world. And one day she—" Then I pinpoint a student with my nearsighted stare and say, "Miss Smith, you take it from there."

And though Miss Smith looks back at me as if she has just seen the Last Judgment, she generally finds she *can* take it from there. Since the story is a communal affair, she isn't afraid of failure, which I think is often the underlying cause when writers can't write. And since the characters are given to her, she doesn't have that feeling so many of us have when facing a blank page: in the beginning was the void, and darkness was upon the face of the page.

Most important, she has a main character whose ruling passion— in this case, a passion for cars—will create the action of the story. And thereby hangs the tale. I have found the experience of telling a story in this way gives us the rare chance to be objective narrators. For once in our lives we are not talking about ourselves.

Let me go back to the woman who loved cars and remind you that characters with an obsession or a passion for something they don't have are common enough in folk tales. "The Juniper Tree," from which I quoted earlier, opens with a woman's overpowering desire to have a child. I could have picked dozens of other examples.

And we all know writers far more sophisticated than the tellers of folk tales who choose to write of such characters. Take, for example, Chekhov's story, "The Man in a Shell," which deals with a character who is obsessed with isolating himself from the world around him. Chekhov describes him as follows:

There are not a few people in the world, temperamentally unsociable, who try to withdraw into a shell like a hermit crab or a snail. . . . Why, not to go far afield, there was Belikov, a colleague of mine, a teacher of Greek, who died in our town about two months ago. You have heard of him, no doubt. The curious thing about him was that he wore rubbers, and a warm coat with an interlining, and carried an umbrella even in the finest weather. And he kept his umbrella in its cover and his watch in a gray chamois case, and when he took out his penknife to sharpen his pencil, his penknife too was in a little case; and his face seemed to be in a case too, because it was always hidden in his turned-up collar. He wore dark spectacles and a sweater, stuffed his ears with cotton-wool, and when he got into a cab always told the driver to put up the hood. In short, the man showed a constant and irrepressible in-clination to keep a covering about himself . . . which would isolate him and protect him from outside influences. Actuality irritated him, frightened him, kept him in a state of continual agitation, and perhaps to justify his timidity, his aversion for the present, he would always laud the past and things that had never existed, and the dead languages that he taught were in effect for him the same rubbers and umbrella in which he sought concealment from real life.[4]

Now why choose such a character for the subject of a story? Because the story begins at the point when such a character meets someone or something that brings him out of his shell. When the man's friends conspire to marry him off, what do you think he does? I will not spoil your pleasure in reading the story by giving away the ending.

I once tried to write a story about a man ruled by a passion for telling lies. I called it "The Tailor Who Told the Truth," because in the last scene, he was cured of his passion for lying, and why hold a penitent man's past failings against him forever? Descriptions of stories are always awkward, so let me quote the opening paragraph:

In Germantown, New York, on Cherry Street, there lived a tailor named Morgon Axel who, out of long habit, could not tell the truth. As a child he told small lies to put a bright surface on a drab life; as a young man he told bigger lies to get what he wanted. He got what he wanted and went on lying until now when he talked about himself, he did not know the truth from what he wanted the truth to be. The stories he told were often more plausible to him than his own life.

I found the process of writing this story very different from writing about my own experience or my immediate observation of someone else's. In the first place, the tailor was born with a peculiar autonomy, a sort of arrogance, as if I hadn't created him at all. He had already selected the details about himself he wished me to know, and I found myself describing places and situations quite foreign to me. The first half of the story is set in Germany before World War I, up to World War II. I have not visited Germany for at least twenty-five years, and my impressions of Germany between these wars come primarily from the old photograph albums kept by my parents, who lived there briefly during the twenties.

My ignorance did not deter the tailor, however. One night I dreamed that the tailor and I, his creator, had an awful row about the direction I wanted the story to go. I told him the plot, the action as I saw it. He told me that I had my story all wrong, it hadn't happened that way at all, and why did I insist on changing the truth?

Well, he won and I wrote the story his way. Let me remind you that "The Tailor Who Told the Truth" is a written story; that is, I did not tell it out loud to a listener and write it down afterward. Though for me there is a close connection between telling and writing, they are, in the end, two different processes. But I believe that the more you tell stories, and the more you listen to stories, the more it will affect the way you write stories.

How?

First, you find yourself creating characters who are not just individuals but also types. I do not mean stereotypes, those unrealized abstractions on which so many stories have foundered. I mean types of people. The misanthrope. The miser. The martyr. The woman who wants a child. The man who lives in a shell. A character who is both an individual and a type is larger than life. Let us call him an archetype; he is some facet of ourselves that we have in common with the rest of humanity.

Second, you find you are not dealing with individual situations but with the forces that created them. I call these forces good and evil, though I would not name them as such in a story. Stories that develop archetypal situations have the truth and the authority of proverbs, no matter how fantastic the particular events they describe.

Third, you find yourself using fewer adjectives and more verbs, because verbs make the story move. You don't develop your character by describing the kind of man he is—a bad man, a good man, an indifferent man; you develop him by showing what he does. It's up to the reader to pass judgment.

Fourth, you the writer become less important than the story you have to tell. And thank heaven for that. Which of us doesn't enjoy telling tall tales where we can lie outrageously without having to justify ourselves?

So far, so good. But we are readers and writers, not storytellers sitting around a fire, spinning tales out of a common heritage. I suppose it's the desire to bring the two together that leads some writers to put a story into the mouth of a narrator, at one remove from the writer himself. In "The Man in the Shell," from which I quoted earlier, Chekhov uses a narrator, so that we have a story within a story.

Let me suggest two reasons for using a narrator to tell your story. First, you may want a limited point of view rather than an omniscient point of view. Second, you may want the economy that a story has when it is told rather than written. Isaac Bashevis Singer once explained to an interviewer why he so often puts his story into the mouth of an old village woman instead of narrating it himself. He says:

Why I like narrators? There is a good reason for that: because when I write a story without a narrator I have to describe things, while if the narrator is a woman she can tell you many things almost in one sentence. Because in life when you sit down to tell a story you don't act like a writer. You don't describe too much. You jump, you digress and this gives to the story speed and drama . . . it comes out especially good when you let an old woman tell a story. In a moment she's here, and a moment she's there. And because of this you feel almost that a human being is talking to you, and you don't need the kind of description which you expect when the writer himself is telling the story.[5]

To illustrate Singer's point, I want to quote from the opening paragraph of one of his stories. It is called "Passions."

"When a man persists he can do things which one might think can never be done," Zalman the glazier said. "In our village, Radoszyce, there was a simple man, a village peddler, Lieb Belkes. He used to go from village to village, selling the peasant women kerchiefs, glass beads, perfume, all kinds of gilded jewelry. And he would buy from them a measure of buckwheat, a wreath of garlic, a pot of honey, a sack of flax. He never went farther than the hamlet of Byszcz, five miles from Radoszyce. He got the merchandise from a Lublin salesman, and the same man bought his wares from him. This Lieb Belkes was a common man but pious. On the Sabbath he read his wife's Yiddish Bible. He loved most to read about the land of Israel. Sometimes he would stop the cheder boys and ask, 'Which is deeper—the Jordan or the Red Sea?' 'Do apples grow in the Holy Land?' 'What language is spoken by the natives there?' The boys used to laugh at him. He looked like someone from the Holy Land himself—black eyes, a pitch-black beard, and his face was also swarthy."[6]

Singer's story is a long way from "The Juniper Tree," but a number of things in that paragraph will show you that their roots grow in the same place, the archetypal obsessions of man. The opening sentence directs me to the point of the story, which, like a fable, demonstrates a simple proverb: the man who persists can do the impossible. The man who wants to go to the Holy Land will find a way to get there.

Singer recognizes that a man's actions are often inseparable from the objects that make up the fabric of his life. He also knows that we cannot see or touch an abstraction. And so he gives us garlic and perfume to smell, and honey and buckwheat to taste, and jewelry and kerchiefs to please the eye, and speech to please the ear. The speech is what I call essential speech in a story; that is, I could recognize this character by his speech later on, even if Singer chose not to identify him. The opposite of essential speech is small talk, which does not directly express a man or woman's deepest needs, but which is really a way of avoiding them.

Now suppose you have resolved to try writing as if you were telling a story. You are ready to simplify your style and to emphasize action and plot more than you may ever wish to do again. But there is one more problem you will have to confront, and I have saved it for the last because it is the most unsettling and, at the same time, the most exhilarating. When you tell a story, you find that without knowing how or why, you cross over easily from the natural to the supernatural as if you felt absolutely no difference between them.

By supernatural, let me hasten to add, I do not mean ghosts, although ghosts of one kind or another may blow through your story and make themselves at home there. I mean the visible, tangible world released from the laws that, in ordinary experience, separate time from place. You know from your own experience that the supernatural is no farther away than your own dreams at night. I do not think there has ever been or ever will be a writer who does not draw on the healing chaos of dreams for the material of stories. Here is a world of wild and fearful happenings, which mercifully vanish when we open our eyes. But occasionally these happenings shine through our daytime lives and illuminate them.

When I am writing stories, I forget that many people do not read fiction, because they believe a book that is neither truthful nor instructive is a waste of time. And fiction, they believe, is not truthful but only made up. It is not instructive but only entertaining. Though my father read stories as a child, when he became a man he put away childish things. He died at the age of ninety-two, he was nearly sixty when I was born, and I believe he read his last piece of fiction in freshman English when he was eighteen. All the years of my growing up, he read nothing of mine except an occasional poem I wrote for his birthday when I didn't have enough money to buy him my standard present of black socks.

Then one day, in his ninetieth year, he picked up a book of my stories and he started to read it. To his astonishment, he found himself in that book, a character in my stories, and like all characters, a fabricated being and yet a real one. In that book I was still trying to describe paradise, but now it was not a place. It was an experience occurring in time but not bound by it.

My father sat in his chair and read. He read one page for an hour. He never said a word to me, he never made a sound, and though he never cried in my presence when I was a child, now the tears were running down his face. He never said, "Stop, I'm there," the way my sister did when we played our game so many years before, but it was the same game nonetheless, and we are all players. It requires two people, the teller and the listener. The teller tells the story he has made out of bits he has seen and pieces he has heard. His telling brings these fragments together, and in that healing synthesis, he gives the wasted hours of our lives an order they don't have and a radiance that only God and the artist can perceive. We get up, we go to work, we come home dead tired, and sometimes we wonder what we are doing on this planet. And we know that in the great schemelessness of things, our own importance is a lie. Is the object of the game to tell that lie? Yes, to tell the lie. But in the telling, to make it true.

NOTES

1. Lore Segal, trans., "The Master Thief," in *The Juniper Tree and Other Tales from Grimm*, vol. I (New York: Farrar, Straus and Giroux, 1973), p. 113.

2. Segal, "The Juniper Tree," vol. 2, p. 314.

3. Segal, "The Juniper Tree," vol. 2, pp. 314–15.

4. Avrahm Yarmolinski, ed., *The Portable Chekhov* (New York: Viking, 1973), pp. 355–56.

5. David M. Andersen, "Isaac Bashevis Singer: Conversations in California," *Modern Fiction Studies*, vol. 16, 1970, p. 436.

6. *Passions and Other Stories* (New York: Farrar, Straus and Giroux, 1975), p. 296.

How Poetry Came into the World and
Why God Doesn't Write It

S E V E R A L months ago I walked into a bookshop determined
not to buy a book and saw, among the remainders, a small volume
called *The Lost Books of Eden*. It beckoned to me like the serpent
poised at the Tree of Knowledge. I considered the price. I considered
my purse. I said to myself, "Opening that book could be dangerous to my economy," and I went out. Instead of leaving the scene of
temptation, I walked around the block. When the bookshop came
into view, I remembered the parable: the kingdom of heaven is like
unto a man seeking goodly pearls who, when he had found one pearl
of great price, went and sold all that he had and bought it. Also,
wisdom is better than rubies, knowledge is better than gold, etc.
Nothing makes us more vulnerable to temptation than ignorance. I
had to know what was in that book.

Alas! When I looked for the book, it was gone. The clerk was
sorry. *The Lost Books of Eden* had just been sold. Since that time I
have speculated on what it might have contained. I have nearly re-
constructed the lost books of Eden in my head. My reconstruction
goes light on doctrine and heavy on losses. I see myself as an insurance salesman. Adam and Eve have found their way to my office.
They draw up two vinyl-covered chairs and tell me their tragedy.
They have lost everything through an act of God.

"Can you be more specific?" I say, shuffling through my papers
for the right forms. "Exactly what did you lose?"

"Eternal life," says Adam.

"The roses I'd just planted in the western bower," says Eve.

"My free time," says Adam.

"My animals," says Eve. "Even the hummingbirds were eating out
of my hand."

"Poetry," says Adam.

"Poetry," says Eve.

"Poetry?" I exclaim. "Well, that's the first thing you've mentioned that *can* be replaced. There's plenty of poetry outside of Eden."

"But it's not the same here as it was there," says Adam. "Poetry was invented in Eden. There was a well in the garden. Any time you put your ear to it, you heard a poem. Anytime you drank from it, you spoke poems. Poetry was so easy. No waiting, no revising, no dry spells."

"Where does the Bible tell how God invented poetry?" I ask.

"God didn't invent it," says Adam. "I did."

"I did too," says Eve. "Remember me?"

"Where does it say so in the Bible?" I demand.

"In the books that were lost," says Adam. "The lost books of Eden. You don't believe me?"

"I don't know what to believe," I answer.

"Look, pretend you're in Eden," says Eve. "God has just spent six days inventing the animals and the birds and the plants, and He's exhausted. He hasn't invented poems; there are some things only humans can make. Unless you want to call the sun and the moon and the birds and the beasts God's poems. Unless you want to call Adam His first reader. The one who's entertained and instructed."

"When God made me in His own image, He made me a creator too," says Adam. "And let me tell you, this creation business interested me a good deal. Especially after God let me name everything. The plants weren't too hard, except there were so many of them. I'd look at a plant and say the first sound that came into my head. And that sound would write itself in letters of gold on the air. Sycamore. Turnip. Gingko. Parsley. Later, in the cool of the evening, God stopped by to see how things were going.

" 'Did you name them all? You didn't forget any of my weeds?'

" 'Not a one,' I told him.

" 'Nice work, Adam,' said God. 'Now I want you to name the animals.'

"One by one, the animals filed by me and waited to see what I would call them. A low beast with pointed ears and long whiskers came by, softly, softly. I said the first sound that came into my head.

" 'Cat.'

"And the name wrote itself on the air in letters of gold: C-A-T.

" 'That's what you think,' said the cat. 'That's what you call me. But it's not what I call myself.'

" 'What do you call yourself?' I asked.

" 'I am he who counteracts the powers of darkness with my electrical skin and glaring eyes,' announced the cat.

"The cat's name for himself also appeared on the air in letters of gold.

" 'To me you're a cat,' I tell him. 'Next!'

"Another small beast hopped up. A beast with long ears and a brief tail. And again I said the first sound that came into my head.

" 'Hare.'

"The name hung in the air for a moment before it floated down to the grass. Nice, short, easy to say.

" 'That's my first name,' said the little beast, 'but not my last.'

" 'What is your last name?'

" 'Which one?' asked the hare. 'There's jumper and racer, there's hug-the-ground and frisky legs, there's long lugs, grass-biter, dew-hammer, race-the-wind, jig-foot—'

" 'Wait!' I exclaimed.

" 'There's creep-along, sitter-still, shake-the-heart, fern-sitter, hedge-squatter—'

"The names were writing themselves in the air like crazy.

" 'You're *hare* to me,' I said.

"The animals took their names politely but they kept their own, and they let me know that those were their real names. At the end of the day, names sparkled in heaps on the grass; the garden was littered with them. I gathered them up and threw them in the well under the Tree of Knowledge. But they didn't sink out of sight. They stuck together, they made new names, they told each other secrets. I could see that Creation was no simple matter.

"So one day I said to God,

" 'Show me how You made some of this stuff. That snake, for example.'

" 'No,' says God. 'Trade secret. I don't give away my trade secrets.'

" 'How about one little secret? A blade of grass, for example. Or that cat sitting in the grass.'

"God considered the cat. He considered it all at once, eternally, from its alpha to its omega.

" 'It's a funny thing,' said God, 'but I don't thrill to it anymore.

Except when you do, Adam. What good is creation if nobody enjoys it?'

" 'I enjoy it.'

" 'Tell me about it,' said God.

"I thought hard. What could I tell God about the grass? I sat at the well and poked around for that word to see what happened to it.

" 'Grass!' I called hopefully.

"To my surprise, the word *grass* swam right up like a fish and stayed there, shimmering. I took a big drink from the well. And that evening when God came by to see how things were, I opened my mouth and the well-words rolled out. Words about the grass.

A child said *What is the grass?* fetching it to me with full hands.
How could I answer the child? I do not know what it is any more than he.
I guess it must be the flag of my disposition, out of hopeful green stuff woven.

> Or I guess it is the handkerchief of the Lord,
> A scented gift and remembrancer designedly dropt,
> Bearing the owner's name someway in the corners, that we
> may see and remark, and say *Whose?*

" 'Nice,' says God. 'That's awfully nice.'

" 'You mean the grass?' I said.

" 'No, the questions. They make me forget I know all the answers. Can you make them work on something else?'

"And God went away. The next evening I looked around the garden and spied a tyger lounging under the Tree of Knowledge. I looked into the well. There, lazing on the surface of the water, gleamed my questions about the grass. I stirred them back down and I leaned close to the water.

" 'Tyger,' I said.

"The word TYGER swam right up, and I took a drink from the well. And that evening God came by to see how I was doing.

" 'I've got some questions for you, God. Questions about the tyger.'

" 'Let's hear them,' says God.

"So I opened my mouth and the well-words rolled out. Words about the tyger.

> Tyger! Tyger! burning bright
> in the forests of the night,

What immortal hand or eye
could frame thy fearful symmetry?

In what distant deeps or skies
Burnt the fire of thine eyes?
On what wings dare he aspire?
What the hand dare seize the fire?

And what shoulder, and what art,
Could twist the sinews of thy heart?
And when thy heart began to beat,
What dread hand? and what dread feet?

What the hammer? what the chain?
In what furnace was thy brain?
What the anvil? What dread grasp
Dare its deadly terrors clasp?

When the stars threw down their spears,
And water'd heaven with their tears,
Did he smile his work to see?
Did he who made the Lamb make thee?

Tyger! Tyger! burning bright
in the forests of the night,
What immortal hand or eye,
Dare frame thy fearful symmetry?

" 'I like it,' says God.

"The tyger liked it too. Said the questions made him seem mysterious and important. For a while everything in the garden wanted me to say questions about it. I made questions about the lion and the rose and the wren and the snake and the lamb; I made questions for all of them. It was 'Little lamb who made thee' and 'Little rose who made thee,' and all the creatures in the garden were happy. And every time I said my questions to God, He nodded.

" 'Nice,' He'd say.

"But I could see that God was getting bored. After all, didn't He make everything? Didn't He know it all from the beginning? So I decided to try something new. I'd let God ask the questions. I'd think of something and give Him a couple of clues, and I'd wrap it in images like a gift in a box. And when God guessed what I was thinking of, the box would open.

"For my first gift, I'd start with the well itself.

"The next evening when God came by to see how I was doing, I said,

> As round as an apple,
> As deep as a cup,
> And all God's horses
> Cannot pull it up.

" 'What are you talking about?' said God.

" 'This well,' I said.

" 'Say it again,' said God.

"I said it again.

" 'Nice,' said God, and He looked all pleased. 'The way you made me see it. The way you made it part apple and part cup. The way you made it important. What do you call this thing?'

"I said the first name that came into my head.

" 'Riddle.'

"For days I went around creation riddling this and riddling that. Leaves, flowers, birds, a stone, an egg. I even riddled an egg.

> In marble walls as white as milk,
> lined with a skin as soft as silk
> within a fountain crystal clear
> a golden apple doth appear.
> No doors are there to this stronghold
> Yet thieves break and steal the gold.

"I could see the hen was pleased, but God was getting a trifle bored. Enough riddles already, I thought. I'll try something else. God liked the way I made the well part apple and part cup, and He liked the way I made the egg part marble and silk, part gold and milk, and part crystal. What was the point of making Him say, 'It's an egg' or 'It's a well'? I could just give Him the part He liked: the part where I linked the egg and the well with other things.

"I murmured "egg" over the well, and up swam the word. There in the depths of the well twinkled my questions about the tyger and the lamb and the lion and the rose and the snake, and they were tangled up with my riddles about the well and the egg and the stone and the leaves and the birds; you could hardly tell where one started and the other left off. The word 'egg' had got so mixed up with other words that I hardly recognized it. It looked as if a dream had rocked it for seven nights running.

"Nevertheless, I took a long cool drink.

"That evening when God found me in the garden, I said,

" 'You remember the riddle about the egg.'

" 'Which one?' asked God. 'Weren't there several?'

" 'The one where it turned into marble walls as white as milk.'

" 'Oh, yes,' said God. 'That was nice.'

" 'Well, I've got another egg for you. But you don't have to find it. You just have to believe it.'

" 'I'm listening,' said God.

"So I opened my mouth and the well-words rolled out.

> In this kingdom
> the sun never sets;
> under the pale oval
> of the sky
> there seems no way in
> or out,
> and though there is a sea here
> there is no tide.
>
> For the egg itself
> is a moon
> glowing faintly
> in the galaxy of the barn,
> safe but for the spoon's
> ominous thunder,
> the first delicate crack
> of lightning.[1]

" 'You just told me the egg is a moon and I believed you,' said God. 'I, Who made the egg and Who made the moon. It's a lie. It's like the lies angels tell.'

" 'What other lies are there?' I asked.

" 'Never mind,' said God. 'What do you call it?'

"I said the first name that came into my head.

" 'Metaphor.'

"And for a long while I was happy. But man cannot live by metaphor alone, or questions, or riddles, or even the names of things. And one evening when God stopped by the garden to see how things were going, I said,

" 'God, I'm depressed. I have this wonderful life in the lovely garden and I'm depressed.'

"God looked at me for a long time. He looked right through me.

" 'You have a well-stocked mind,' He said. 'But your heart is empty. You need a helpmate.'

" 'Sounds good to me,' I said. 'When will it arrive?'

" 'Making you a helpmate isn't as simple as making a worm or a wren,' said God. 'Adam, I'm going to give you the first general anesthesia.'

"And God caused me to fall into a deep sleep. And when my body was asleep, my spirit climbed out and flew straight to the well, and jumped in, and came back with all this stuff that the well had made down in the depths. Emerald winds. Tiger lilies. So now I knew how God made things. God wasn't the only one who could dream. God wasn't the only one who could invent. But He was the only one who could bring it all back.

"In the first fragile moments between waking and sleeping, I thought I had brought something back, perhaps a little corner of the emerald wind, speaking in wild green syllables. What I heard on waking was neither bird nor bell nor angel, and it sounded like nothing else in Eden.

> I will give my love an apple without any core,
> I will give my love a house without any door,
> I will give my love a palace wherein he may be
> and he may unlock it without any key.

" 'What's that marvelous sound?' I exclaimed.

" 'That's singing,' said God.

"How can I say what the singing was like? It was not like words rising from the well into my mouth. It was as if the well itself were singing. And hearing that sound for the first time in my life, I was— for the first time in my life—lonely. The singing changed course, the way a river does, but it did not end.

> O, western wind, when wilt thou blow
> that the small rain down may rain?
> Christ, that my love were in my arms
> and I in his bed again!

"I sprang up, wide awake now. And God took my hand and said, " 'Adam, meet Eve. This is your helpmate.'

"She sang *lullay, lullay,* and the birds and beasts tucked their heads under their wings and slept, and she sang Hallelujah! and everything woke up full of praise. Nobody had ever made those words before. She sang, and the words answered with rhythms of their own. One

was like a heartbeat, another like a dance step. As I recognized the
different rhythms, I knew that without realizing it, I'd been hearing
them since the day I was born. I tried to name them, so I could ask
for the ones I liked best. Iamb. Anapest. Trochee. I'd say to Eve, 'Sing
me something in anapests.'

" 'You mean something that sounds like a stone skipping?'

"Sometimes in the middle of her song she'd throw in *lullay, lullay*
or *hey nonny nonny* or *fiddle dee dee*. And I'd look all over creation
for a nonny or a dee, and finally I'd have to ask her, 'What's a fiddle?
What's a dee? What's a nonny?' And she'd laugh and say,

" 'I don't know. It's what the well sings to itself early in the morning. Ask the well.'

"Oh, when she laughed! The stars in their spheres started humming, the morning stars sang together. What were riddles and metaphors to her? She could never remember the names of the iambs and
anapests. But let her draw a song around the simplest thing in the
world, and I would be filled with joy. And long after I'd forgotten
the tune, long after I'd forgotten the words, I could still hear the
rhythm of the words, the hum they make when they dance and sing
in the well. Who can explain singing? It is a bell weeping and it is
a procession of butterflies chanting and it is the tender tread of an
elephant walking in its sleep. And whenever I heard Eve singing, I
said to myself, 'Though I have the secret names of the angels, if I
have not music, I have nothing.' Whenever I made metaphors, I tried
to please the ear of God as well as His eye."

Adam stopped talking. It was very quiet in my office. Even the jani-
tor had gone home. I cleared my throat and shuffled my papers and
tried to remember why I'd ended up in the insurance business. The
reasons eluded me, and I resolved to start looking for another job
tomorrow. Eve blew her nose and wiped her eyes.

"Everyone liked my singing," said Eve, "except the serpent. He'd
come by in the morning and listen to me, though. There was one
song he always asked for, a song I'd sing when I was off tending the
roses in the western bower. I sang it so Adam would know where to
find me.

> It is late last night the dog was speaking of you;
> the snipe was speaking of you in her deep marsh.
> It is you are the lonely bird through the woods;
> and that you may be without a mate until you find me.

"One evening when I sang that song for the serpent, he said,

" 'It's nice. But something is missing. You sing everything in the same key.'

" 'Key?'

" 'Key,' said the serpent. 'Key is what locks the tune to itself and locks it into your heart. You are singing in the key of C major.'

" 'What other key is there?' I asked.

" 'Why, there are more keys for tunes than roses on that bush. When you've found all the major keys, you haven't even started to discover the noble sorrows of the minor keys. Let me sing your song in one of the minor keys and you'll see what you're missing.

When I go by myself to the Well of Loneliness,
I sit down and I go through my trouble;
when I see the world and do not see my boy,
he that has an amber shade in his hair.

My heart is as black as the blackness of the sloe,
or as the black coal that is on the smith's forge;
or as the sole of a shoe left in white halls;
it was you put that darkness over my life.

You have taken the east from me; you have taken the west from me;
you have taken what is before me and what is behind me;
you have taken the moon, you have taken the sun from me;
and my fear is great that you have taken God from me!

"Well, I shivered all over when I heard how the serpent's singing changed things. It was just as if somebody had opened a door in the garden and showed us what we were going to do tomorrow and tomorrow and tomorrow, just as if we could know what only God knew, that our little garden was called out of a sea of darkness, and it could be called back to that darkness. I'd never thought much about the Void, though God had told us a little about how it was before the garden came, when darkness covered the face of the deep.

" 'Wise serpent, wily serpent,' I whispered, 'what is the secret of your singing?'

" 'Loss,' hissed the serpent. 'Change. Sorrow. You and Adam live forever in Eden. When he's gone, you don't miss him. You just misplace him.'

" 'And where can I get loss, change, and sorrow?' I begged.

" 'From the Tree of Knowledge,' replied the serpent.

" 'God said if we eat of that tree we shall surely die,' I said.

"The serpent laughed his flat little breathy laugh.

" 'Did God tell you what death means?' he asked.

" 'He said something about falling asleep forever,' I said. 'To tell you the truth, I didn't pay very much attention.'

" 'Believe me, you won't fall asleep,' the serpent assured me. 'I know. I've eaten from the tree myself. You will be more alive than ever. You will savor every moment. And you will sing the song that makes your bones shiver and your spirit ache with longing.'

" 'But will we fall asleep forever after the song is sung?' I asked.

" 'Eve,' said the serpent, 'you will turn into the greatest gift the tree can offer. Your life will have a beginning and an end. Your life will be a story in the mouths of millions.'

" 'Story,' I repeated. It wasn't a word I knew. 'Did you find that word in the well?'

" 'I put it there myself,' replied the serpent.

" 'And what does a story look like?' I asked.

" 'Like me,' said the serpent. 'I am the very shape of a story. Story is the thread on which all the other words are strung. It pulls them along, it gives them a purpose in life.'

" 'Is it as good as singing? Is it as good as metaphor?' I asked.

" 'My dear little Eve, story is the river on which metaphor moves and has its being. But it can only live in the fullness of time. That's why God, who lives outside of time, can't tell stories. To Him the alpha and the omega, the once-upon-a-time and the happily-ever-after, are features on a single face. But you, Eve, shall tell stories. When you have eaten the fruit of the Tree of Knowledge, you shall know the beginning of your life but not the end of it, only that it must end. You'll tell stories whose endings will surprise you, though you are their teller and creator. The Tree of Knowledge will make you wonderfully ignorant.'

" 'And can I sing stories?' I asked.

" 'Your most beautiful stories will be those you sing,' the serpent assured me. 'And when you sing them, broken lives and broken promises will become as lovely and whole as a tear of crystal.'

" 'Sing me a story,' I begged the serpent. 'Sing me a story made of such healing.'

"So the serpent sang,

> There lived a wife at Usher's Well,
> And a wealthy wife was she;

She had three stout and stalwart sons,
   And sent them o'er the sea.

They hadna been a week from her,
   A week but barely ane,
When word came to the carline wife
   That her three sons were gane.

They hadna been a week from her,
   A week but barely three,
When word came to the carline wife
   That her sons she'd never see.

"I wish the wind may never cease
   Nor fashes in the flood,
Till my three sons come hame to me,
   In earthly flesh and blood."

It fell about the Martinmass,
   When nights are lang and mirk,
The carline wife's three sons came hame,
   and their hats were o' the birk.

It neither grew in syke nor ditch,
   Nor yet in ony sheugh;
But at the gates o Paradise,
   That birk grew fair enough.

"Blow up the fire, my maidens!
   Bring water from the well!
For a' my house shall feast this night,
   Since my three sons are well."

And she has made to them a bed,
   She's made it large and wide,
And she's ta'en her mantle her about,
   Sat down at the bed-side.

Up then crew the red, red cock,
   And up and crew the gray;
The eldest to the youngest said,
   " 'Tis time we were away."

The cock he hadna craw'd but once,
   And clapp'd his wings at a',
When the youngest to the eldest said,
   "Brother, we must awa'.

"The cock doth craw, the day doth daw,
   The channerin' worm doth chide;
Gin we be mist out o' our place,
   A sair pain we maun bide.

"Fair ye weel, my mother dear!
Fareweel to barn and byre!
And fare ye weel, the bonny lass
That kindles my mother's fire!"

" 'I don't understand the story,' I said, 'but I believe it. What's it about?'

" 'It's about you,' said the serpent. 'The wife is you, the maids are you, the lassie by the fire is you. They're all you. When you have eaten the fruit of the Tree of Knowledge, little Eve, no story will be closed to you.'

" 'Give me knowledge,' I pleaded.

" 'What God calls knowledge I call ignorance,' said the serpent. 'What God calls ignorance, I call story. Help yourself to an apple from the tree that stands in the center of the garden.' "

Silence again fell over the three of us. It would be getting dark outside the office, I thought. I don't have a window; you don't get a window till someone who has one quits or dies.

"So you ate the apple, Madam, and you gave a piece to your husband, and God put you both out of the garden with nothing but your fig leaves," I said, trying to sum up the legalities of the case. "You wish to declare a total loss?"

"No," said Adam, "because we didn't lose everything. When the avenging angel took us to the East Gate, just before he opened it, he turned and said to me,

" 'You lost eternal life. How could you be so dumb?'

" 'Eternal life never seemed that great,' I said humbly. 'We'd never known anything else. What I really hate to lose is that well.'

"The angel looked surprised.

" 'Why, that's the only thing you haven't lost,' he said. 'God doesn't want the well. What use is it to God? So He's letting you take it with you.'

" 'Where is it?' I asked.

" 'The well is inside you,' replied the angel. 'Much more convenient to carry it that way. Of course it's not going to be as easy to find as it was in the garden, when you could just lean over and take a drink. Sometimes you'll forget the words you're looking for, or you'll call and the wrong ones will answer. Sometimes they'll be a long time coming. But everything the well gave you it will give you again. Or if not to you, to your children. Or your great-great-great-great-grandchildren. And since God created you in His image, you have His dream power. By the grace of dreams we may meet again, blown together by an emerald wind. And I hope you'll remember me with metaphors and make a lovely web of words about me. I hope you'll make some marvelous—what do you call it?'

"I said the first word that came into my head: 'Poetry.' "

NOTE

"The Egg" is from *PM/AM: New and Selected Poems* (Norton), by Linda Pastan.

Telling Time

O N C E upon a time I received an advertisement in the mail for the complete stories of Chekhov, translated by Constance Garnett. The advertisement informed me that I would receive the first volume free, to get me hooked, and one volume every three months for three years, at the end of which I would own the complete Chekhov. Over seven hundred stories.

Seven hundred stories! I thought. Chekhov was a doctor. Any writer juggling the demands of a job, a novel-in-progress, and a family will probably ask, "How did he find the time to write seven hundred stories?" After I asked the question, I realized that how Chekhov found time for writing was less important to me than how I could find it. Looking for answers, I began to keep track of how I spent my time as a writer.

SEPTEMBER 4

I took out my notes for a new story. Mostly notes on characters. I feel as nervous starting out as if I were going to a party where I don't know anybody. Will I like these characters? Will they like me? Will they tell me their secrets?

I could make an outline of the story I want to tell, but my characters don't like outlines. If I let them unfold in the writing itself, they'll reveal themselves in more interesting ways than my outline could ever have imagined for them. Getting to know your characters is like throwing a block party; you start with a few people, and suddenly the whole neighborhood shows up.

I've started the story with a conversation between the two main characters, by way of introducing them.

SEPT. 10

Today I met with my old friend and former editor at Harcourt Brace Jovanovich, Barbara Lucas, to discuss *The Firebrat*, a fantasy novel I've almost finished. It was inspired by a painting of David Weisner's, in which a boy and a girl emerge from the New York subway to find themselves in a kingdom where fish swim through the air and houses grow on trees. The character I call the Firebrat has nothing to do with David's painting. He's a six-foot scorpion and as pleasant as poison ivy.

Barbara liked the fantasy sections of the book but felt the scenes in the subway were vague. When my writing is vague, it's because I don't know enough about my subject. I need more concrete details. She also felt the character of the magician needs more work.

"What does he look like?" she asked. "All you've given your reader is dialogue."

I'm determined to spend an entire day riding the New York subway.

SEPT. 16

Dinner last night with Alice and Martin Provensen. Throughout the meal a golden retriever sat by Martin's chair and rested its head on his knee, the very image of canine devotion. The Provensens' farm is my idea of what the peaceable kingdom looks like. Horses in a field, a boisterous rooster, any number of cats, a tribe of hens whom Martin has nicknamed the Thurbers, and a crotchety goose named Evil Murdoch. Martin told us that one fine fall day when the wild geese were flying and calling high overhead, Evil Murdoch was seen walking down the turnpike headed south.

At dinner we talked about plans for their daughter Karen's wedding, we talked about the naming of animals, we talked about everything except the one subject I was dying to bring up: the illustrations for the new book we're doing together, *The Voyage of the Ludgate Hill*. Though I'd love to see some sketches, Alice and Martin are as secretive as alchemists about what they're working on, especially toward the author. "If you showed in your face that you didn't like what we were doing, we would find it hard to go back to the drawing board in the same spirit we left it," Martin told me once.

It seems ages ago that they sent me a small volume of Robert

Louis Stevenson's letters, asking if I could write a poem for them to illustrate based on a letter he wrote to Henry James in 1887. In that letter, Stevenson describes his voyage from London to New York on the good ship *Ludgate Hill.*

I . . . enjoyed myself more than I could have hoped on board our strange floating menagerie: stallions and monkeys and matches made up our cargo; and the vast continent of these incongruities rolled the while like a haystack; and the stallions stood hypnotised by the motion, looking through the ports at our dinner-table, and winked when the crockery was broken; and the little monkeys stared at each other in their cages . . . ; and the big monkey, Jacko, scoured about the ship and rested willingly in my arms, to the ruin of my clothing . . . and the other passengers, where they were not sick, looked on and laughed. Take all this picture, and make it roll till the bell shall sound unexpected notes and the fittings shall break loose in our stateroom, and you have the voyage of the *Ludgate Hill.*" (*The Letters of Robert Louis Stevenson*, ed. Sir Sidney Colvin, New York: Charles Scribner's Sons, 1925, p. 7

SEPT. 25

While browsing in a secondhand shop, I came across a garden magazine intended for an audience of gardeners richer than I. Such wonderful articles telling you how to landscape your fifty acres with fountains, walls, terraces, etc. In the middle of an article on the Hellbrun palace in Salzburg, something took hold of me, some odd twist of association, and I heard one of my characters talking to herself. The most important thing for me, at this stage, is to get the voice right. The voice of whoever is telling the story.

I haven't a clue as to how my story will end. But that's all right. When you set out on a journey and night covers the road, you don't conclude that the road has vanished. And how else could we discover the stars?

OCTOBER 1

I spent the afternoon riding the New York subway. The train did not break down, an army of muggers did not set upon me with sticks, a fat man did not step on my feet, I did not get stuck in the turnstile, and the hole in my pocket did not send dimes and nickels and subway tokens spinning to the pavement.

This isn't to say that nothing happened. I have always liked Rilke's description of what happens when nothing is happening:

Who can name you all, you confederates of inspiration, you who are no more than sounds or bells that cease, or wonderfully new bird-voices in the neglected woods, or shining light thrown by an opening window out into the hovering morning; or cascading water; or air; or glances. Chance glances of passers-by . . . behold; they beckon here, and the divine line passes over them into the eternal. ("The Young Poet," *Selected Works: Vol. I, Prose*, Norfolk, Connecticut: New Directions, 1960, pp. 60–61)

I came away with nothing so grand as a divine line passing over into the eternal, but I did meet an itinerant singer who was so like my idea of the magician in *Firebrat* that I almost thought I'd conjured him up. A starfish in his lapel, a moustache like the tusks of a walrus, fingers agleam with rings as he picked out "The Golden Vanity" on his guitar.

When I set about rewriting the subway scene in my manuscript, I knew what was missing. I'd mentioned the roar of the subway but not the silence and not the far-off drip drip drip of water seeping through the walls. I'd shown the jumble of graffiti on the cars but not the bleak space across the empty platforms after the train has left.

The magician in this book will look like the itinerant subway singer.

OCT. 10

I sent *Firebrat* to my agent, who called to say she will submit it to Random House.

Back to my story. Worked on it last night and dreamed over it this morning. That twilight state between dreaming and waking is a good time for watching the story work itself out. I say watching, because it really is like watching an animal, tracking it, understanding it, and finally training it.

By the harsh light of day I re-read the two pages of conversation that open the story. Now they seem to me as clumsy as the opening scene in one of those melodramas, in which the maid and the butler meet in the living room and discuss all the circumstances that have led up to the present crisis. The master has been away, the mistress is ill, the mistress's brother has gambled away the family fortune, etc. Naturally you never meet the maid and the butler again. Why should you? They're not characters, they're mouthpieces for conveying information.

I spent the morning groping for a way of dramatizing the information my reader will need to get on with my story. Well, I'm not writing a newspaper article. I don't need to give all the particulars of who, what, when, and where, in the first paragraph. Isn't knowing when to withhold information one of the hard-won secrets of writing fiction? Did Stephen Crane worry about giving information when he wrote the opening sentence of "The Open Boat"?

"Nobody knew the color of the sky."

I want my opening sentence to let the reader know, as unobtrusively as possible, what kind of story he or she is spending time with. Realistic? Fantasy? When D. H. Lawrence opens a story with "There was a man who loved islands. He was born on one, but it didn't suit him, as there were too many other people on it, besides himself," I know right away that I'm in the presence of an extended parable.

OCT. 14

A new building is going up in our neighborhood. The sign in front gives it a working title, "Future Home of Zimmer Brothers' Jewelry Store." Since I pass it every morning on my way to buy the paper, I've seen the foundation poured, the girders laid, the walls rising. At this stage, it looks like an empty swimming pool. Early one morning, before the regular crew had arrived, I saw a man standing at the bottom, all alone, unrolling a scroll. He was dressed like a workman with one curious exception: instead of a yellow hardhat, he wore a visored cap with silver wings and his glance rested on empty space, as if he were about to perform a miracle. Building Rome in a day.

Two days later a drawing board stood on that very spot. On the drawing board lay the plans for the miracle. I felt as if I were looking at a gigantic metaphor for the way writers construct stories.

I've studied the plans for my story—they're all over my desk—but I haven't seen a man in a winged cap at the heart of it all. But I'm hoping for one—or maybe a winged lady, a sort of Winged Victory—who can convert my rough draft into a miracle.

Several years ago I read an article by Gail Godwin in which she suggested that having a mental picture of one's muse is very useful for overcoming writer's block. I tried it and discovered I had not one muse but two. Two sisters, one obsessively shy and the other obsessively tidy. The shy one was unavailable; she was always off walking in the woods. But the tidy one told me about her. Said she likes to sit under a certain pine tree looking for bones. An owl who lives in the tree eats dozens of mice every night, and every night he throws their bones away. A mouse's bones are no bigger than the gears in a watch. The shy sister makes whistles of them so they'll sing when she breathes through them. The tidy sister is not fond of bones. The forest is her living room, and she can't bear to have mouse bones in her living room. She cleans and prunes and edits. Sometimes I want one sister, sometimes the other. But if I have writer's block, I know it's because the tidy sister is scolding the trees for growing and the milkweed for blowing, and then I hang out a sign for her. DEAR MADAM: I APPRECIATE YOUR SERVICES BUT PLEASE DO NOT COME TILL YOU ARE CALLED. I can't have her around in the beginning when my poem or story is feeling its way into leaf and flower.

Finished three pages on my story. It's about a woman whose husband keeps changing jobs. Her great desire is to live in one place long enough to put down roots.

OCT. 16

A day of distractions. The cat has an abscessed tooth, the cold water faucet is broken in the bathroom, the light doesn't work in the cellar, and I've spent the morning on the telephone, pleading with plumbers and electricians. When I look at my manuscript, I feel I've lost the thread of the narrative. I have to resist the temptation to pile up page after page, to prove to myself that I am indeed writing. When I stop and ask myself, What is the story? I can't give myself a straight answer.

There's only one cure: to put the story on the back burner and turn to something else. I've always wanted to write a poem on our local hardware store—it's such a paragon of order and completeness. Bins of nails, screws, latches for every purpose under heaven. Would that there were such a store for writers. Bins of opening lines, transitions, closing sentences—it's just a matter of finding the one that fits.

When I tried to start the poem, I discovered I didn't even know the names of half the things I'd been seeing for years. I spent the afternoon at the hardware store, looking and learning. A careful examination of the commonplace is, for me, one of the best ways of keeping in touch with the man in the winged cap—or the shy sister in the forest.

OCT. 18

Maria Modugno, my editor at Harcourt Brace Jovanovich, called to say that she is coming east. She'll stop at Alice and Martin's, pick up the illustrations for *Ludgate Hill*, and stay the night in Poughkeepsie with us.

OCT. 20

Eric told me a curious anecdote about an electrical engineer he knows at work, who is taking early retirement so he can devote full time to his writing. He came to writing many years ago with no background in literature at all. "All my life," he told Eric, "I saw the world so differently from the way my friends saw it that I figured I must be a little crazy." The difference had something to do with imagination and intuition, though at the time he didn't use those words to explain it.

One day he picked up a copy of the *New Yorker* in a doctor's office and read the first story. "If I'm crazy," he told himself, "the guy who wrote this story is crazy in the same way I am."

He read the next story and the next with growing excitement, and on the way home from the doctor's office, he mailed his subscription to the *New Yorker* and eagerly awaited the first issue. He read every issue from cover to cover, and one day he sat down to write a story of his own.

The writing went smoothly enough, but having finished his story, he did not know how to submit it. So he called the *New Yorker* to find out. The receptionist was amused and patient.

"You put the story in an envelope," she explained, "and you include return postage. And then you wait for an answer."

He waited. He waited for six months. He waited the way we have all waited. After six months, he called the magazine. The kind receptionist told him a letter was in the mail. Two days later he received the letter. The *New Yorker* wanted to buy his story. He was ecstatic. How many people sell their first story to the *New Yorker*?

But his second and third stories did not fare so well. They came back bearing notes from Rachel MacKenzie, an editor known for her candor. "This stinks."

I can't help thinking of what a friend of mine said when I congratulated him on the acceptance of his first novel. "Now I'm trying to start the second one. I thought it would be easier. Well, it's not. I'm right back in square one."

OCT. 28

Maria Modugno, my editor at HBJ, arrived yesterday evening, and we arranged the artwork for *Ludgate Hill* in the living room, on the sofa and along the walls, and then we ooh'd and ah'd. She told me that when she arrived at their studio, Alice and Martin were frowning at the page on which a lively baboon makes its first appearance.

"It needs a little more blue," said Alice.

Martin picked up his brush and added a single stroke. Turning to Maria, Alice gave Martin a compliment that came from forty-two years of being happily married and making fifty-six books together.

"Nobody paints baboons better than Martin," said Alice.

Maria spent the night on our living room sofa. At midnight a huge raccoon tried to batter his way through the cat door. At two in the morning the cat himself began playing the piano by walking up and down on the keys. I fear she will never accept our hospitality again.

I finished the poem on the hardware store.

> *A Hardware Store as Proof of the Existence of God*
> I praise the brightness of hammers pointing east
> like the steel woodpeckers of the future,
> and dozens of hinges opening brass wings,
> and six new rakes shyly fanning their toes,
> and bins of hooks glittering into bees,
>
> and a rack of wrenches like the long bones of horses,
> and mailboxes sowing rows of silver chapels,
> and a company of plungers waiting for God
> to claim their thin legs and walk away laughing.
>
> In a world not perfect but not bad either
> let there be glue, glaze, gum, and grabs,
> calk also, and hooks, shackles, cables, and slips,
> and signs so spare a child may read them,
> *Men, Women, In, Out, No Parking, Beware the Dog.*
>
> In the right hands, they can work wonders.

NOVEMBER I

Something there is that doesn't love a word, and it took up residence in the word processor I'm learning—with difficulty—how to use. I had got all the way up to page nineteen of my story when the screen flashed a message, DISK ERROR. Sentences slid into gibberish, words collapsed into cuneiform. The last line I'd written began pulsing like a mad neon sign. I exited, as the expression goes, turned off the machine, and fled downstairs to make a cup of coffee. When I returned to my story, half an hour later, all but three lines were gone.

Immediately I put in a new disk and wrote out as much as I could remember of what I'd lost. A few hours later, I sat down at the PC and summoned up my hastily written memories of those lost pages. Gone. I'm unspeakably depressed.

NOV. 2

I rose at dawn and wrote out my story for the third time, and for the third time, it vanished. Eric and I spent the day trying to diagnose the problem. If machines were murderable, this one would be dead. I've gone back to the 1936 Smith Corona that I bought for twenty-four dollars in a secondhand shop. Like a faithful family retainer, it runs without complaint. Naturally I'm forced to write more slowly. But this has its advantages. When you write slowly, you give the odd associations that hang around the edges of a scene their due. It's like zipping through the countryside in a limousine that suddenly breaks down. I have to get out and walk, and that's when I discover the chicory, the wild grapevine, and the ten different species of wild grasses.

To write fast enough and at the same time to write slowly enough —isn't that the paradox at the heart of the writer's dilemma about finding time? This afternoon when I was in the library, the title of an article in *The Writer's Digest* caught my eye: "How to Write Fast." I picked up the magazine and leafed through it and found myself diverted by a list of books deemed useful for writers. *Writing the Novel: From Plot to Print, How to Write While You Sleep . . . and Other Surprising Ways to Increase Your Writing Power, How to Stop Snoring, Make Your House Do the Housework, How to Find Another Husband . . . By Someone Who Did, Writing after Fifty, Waking Up Dry: How to End Bedwetting Forever.*

You could buy a laminated walnut writer's block if you sent fifteen dollars to the right party. A sort of voodoo item, I guess; you could pass it on to the writer who gives you a bad review.

I suppose we all want to write faster. At our backs we hear time's winged chariot, and when we try to set ourselves schedules for writing, it's because writing is work, and nobody can do this work for us.

But finding time isn't enough. It must be the right kind of time, and the right kind of time is as hard to find as truffles or wild orchids. The time by which the man in the winged cap and the shy sister in the forest live—that's the kind I want. And that kind of time knows nothing about schedules. It's close to what one scholar of native American art has described as the Indian sense of time.

It teaches the great lesson of patience, and in this it commands respect . . . Although Indians say nothing about it, the artistic part of their culture is . . . created in the framework of ceremonial time—slow time . . . Pueblo clay can only be gathered when conditions are right and after prayers are said . . . While creating, they are inside time and react to an internal rhythm that cannot be talked about, but which is nevertheless there. Ceremonial time is private time. Many craft workers do not like to be observed while working, and the firing of Pueblo pottery is mostly done in secret. (Ralph T. Coe, *Lost and Found Traditions, Native American Art 1965–1985*, Seattle: University of Washington Press, in association with the American Federation of Arts, 1986)

NOV. 4

My agent called to say that Random House wants to buy *Firebrat*. Janet Schulman, the editor, wants numerous revisions, and she has offered to come to Poughkeepsie so that we can discuss them. Oh, I hoped she'd think it was perfect. Sometimes I think all I want is to be praised.

I hate to interrupt the story I'm doing now to tinker with a book I let go of months ago. When a book is finished, the connection between me and the characters is broken. In a year or two I'll have forgotten their names. They become like the people you meet on a trip. You send them Christmas cards till you realize you can't recall what they look like.

NOV. 23

A good friend has just been accepted for a three-week stint at the Virginia Colony of the Arts. Concentration, a gift of time; it does wonders for your writing, he assured me.

I suppose it does. But I'd miss the connection with everyday life— my son coming home at three, telling tales out of school. Like the one about the science teacher who keeps dead mice in his freezer to feed his pet boa constrictor. One day when the snake looked particularly famished, he popped a frozen mouse into the microwave. A small grey explosion followed. There are no oven-cleaning compounds on the market guaranteed to banish entrails of mouse.

Stories, stories. What does a writer do? I like William Carlos Williams's answer. *I listen. This is my entire occupation.*

DECEMBER 10

Today Janet Schulman came to Poughkeepsie and we went over the manuscript of *Firebrat*. Right off, she wanted me to change the title, and I felt like my immigrant relatives from Sweden who lost their good family name somewhere on Ellis Island. "Too many Martinsons here already," snapped an official. "From now on, your name is Hedlund."

It seems that Simon and Schuster is coming out with a series of young adult books called *The Firebrats*, about teenagers after a nuclear disaster.

"How about calling it *The Quest for Firebrat?*" suggested Janet.

"Quest" is a word I abhor. What if Lewis Carroll had called his book *Alice's Quest for Wonderland?* What if L. Frank Baum had called his *Dorothy's Quest for the Emerald City?* To me, "Quest" suggests a pale imitation of King Arthur, a pasteboard medieval story.

So my title will have to stay.

Her other suggestions were fine. The skill of a good editor never fails to amaze me—that perfect blend of severity and understanding. Janet reminds me of pleasant-faced Mrs. Bowman, who worked in the AAA office in Ann Arbor. Every summer when I was in high school our family drove from Ann Arbor, Michigan, to Albuquerque, New Mexico, where my father was teaching summer school. A week before the trip, he'd sit down with Mrs. Bowman, and with much folding and refolding of maps, they would discuss the dangers and possibilities. The cities where it was easy to get lost. The towns where you could see notable attractions. My father did not care for museums, but he was never in such a hurry that he wouldn't stop to see something advertised—usually on a hand-lettered sign in the middle of the desert—as a notable attraction. The crater left by a falling star. The rattlesnake that killed the mayor's wife in a town so small you could blink twice and miss it altogether. Never mind that the notable attractions we saw were notable to nobody else. When he left the AAA office, he carried a book of strip maps with our route carefully marked in red.

Years later, sitting in on one of John Gardner's workshops at Bread Loaf, I thought of those strip maps. John was telling how he kept track of details when he worked on a long novel. Shelf paper, he said. You unwind the roll, you tape it to the four walls of your room. You divide it into chapters, leaving plenty of space between them, because you'll soon be filling those spaces with notes. You could call it a map to help you navigate the unknown waters of your novel-in-progress. But never forget that you're in charge of the terrain. After all, you invented it. If that wonderful cleaning woman you so casually introduced in chapter three keeps trying to take over the story, you just might want to change the map.

Janet did have a few misgivings about the character of the magician. "Some of the details you use to describe him don't connect with anything else in the book," she remarked.

I started to tell her that it was all true, I'd seen this wonderful itinerant singer in the subway—and then I stopped. Oh, I've succumbed to one of the writer's strongest temptations: the wish to include something because it really happened. How often, when I've told a student that a scene is not convincing, do I hear the indignant outcry, "But it really happened!" Whether it happened to you doesn't matter. Whether the reader believes it happened—that's what matters.

Why can't I follow my own advice?

DEC. 27

Eric and James and I spent the Christmas holidays zipping between Ann Arbor and Grosse Pointe and Toledo, visiting our mothers and other relatives. Yesterday Eric and James returned home. I'm staying in Ann Arbor over the New Year to take care of Mother. She's had what the doctor calls a series of "small strokes." Small to him, maybe, but not to her. At a stroke she's lost some of her most precious memories, and hoping to find them again, she asks the same questions over and over. *Did I have a wedding? Is my sister still alive? How did my mother die?*

When darkness falls, a nameless anxiety overtakes her. Her doctor calls it "the sundown syndrome." All night long she goes up and down the stairs, checking to see if the doors are locked, peeking into every room in the house. "Who's staying with me? Whose house is this?" she asks. "Am I alone? Did I sleep here last night?" She dreamed that somebody kidnapped her and held her for ransom.

Sleep is impossible for both of us. She sleeps so lightly. Every ten minutes she comes into my room and turns on the light on the pretext of bringing me something.

At two A.M. she lugged in a huge portrait of my grandfather. At three A.M. she was standing by my bed holding her college diploma. "Do you know where your diploma is?" she asked.

When she finally went to bed at four, I fell asleep and dreamed that all the cars in Ann Arbor had identical bumperstickers. *It's three* A.M. *Do you know where your diploma is?*

DEC. 30

After four nights of not getting to sleep before four in the morning I feel like a zombie. Sunday when I tried to wake Mother up for church, she threatened to call the humane society and report me. I was determined to get her out of the house. We made it to church in time for the closing benediction. Mother turned to me and said, "That's the shortest service I've ever heard in my life."

Border's bookshop was open. We stopped to browse. I bought Troyat's biography of Chekhov to read while Mother is roaming around the house at night. Last night around three A.M. she brought me some literature left by the Jehovah's Witnesses: a magazine called *Awake* and a book called *How to Get into Paradise.*

DEC. 31 / 86

New Year's Eve. We are watching old Cary Grant movies and the news and the weather. Over and over, the same news, the same weather.

I've started reading the Chekhov biography by the flickering light of the TV and feel humbled. The description of his life in Moscow during a typhus epidemic puts my sleepless nights into perspective.

Like all doctors he was constantly on call, and he slept only a few hours a night. . . . Even when he could grab a bit of time from his patients, he had trouble concentrating on the blank page. An entire floor of the building where he lived was occupied by a caterer, who used it for wedding receptions, funeral dinners, and guild banquets, and the shouting, the blare of music, the tinkle of dishes never seemed to end. To Bilibin he wrote: "There is a wedding orchestra playing over my head at the moment . . . Some asses are getting married and stomping away like horses"; and to Leikin: "I've been so exhausted, frenzied and crazed these past two weeks that my head is spinning. . . . The flat is constantly full of people, noise, music. . . . The office is cold. . . . The patients keep coming. . . ." (*Chekhov*, Henry Troyat, translated from the French by Michael Henry Heim, New York: E. P. Dutton, 1986, pp. 69–70)

Who am I to complain about one ailing mother?

JANUARY 3 / 87

Last night I took the train back to Poughkeepsie. As I stepped up to the ticket window to ask when my train was leaving, I was clutching the Chekhov biography. The ticket-taker looked at it and smiled.

"Chekhov! Hey, you a Star Trek fan?"

FEBRUARY 27

Tying up the newspapers for recycling, I fell to reading old Sunday magazine sections of the *New York Times*. How could I have missed the issue with the photograph of Joan Didion in her study in California? Her window faces the ocean, her desk is so vast she could tapdance on it. A room of her own, full of purpose, and space, and light.

My study, which I share with my son, James, commands a fine view of Craven's funeral parlor. On a busy day, they do as many as eight funerals over there. The mourners arrive, the hearses gather them up. When the last hearse has vanished, Mrs. Craven runs outside and hangs up her laundry. When the next batch of mourners arrives, she takes it all down again. Sometimes at night an ambulance comes, its lights flashing.

It is nearly midnight. Eric is working in his darkroom, and in the next room, James is reading a new Phil Dick novel; a repetitive tune—I think it's something from a tape of the "Grateful Dead"— drifts through the closed door. All this coming and going does sharpen one's sense of time. How it passes.

MARCH 29

This afternoon—a warm Sunday, the daffodils are nodding, the tulips are sending up brilliant globes to light the shady beds of violets—this afternoon I got a call from a friend of Alice and Martin Provensen.

"I wanted to tell you this before you read it in the newspaper," she said. "Martin died of a heart attack on Friday morning."

I was so stunned that I hardly heard her account of how it happened. He'd stepped outside and raised his hand to hail the man who was picking up fallen brush. Was Martin greeting him? Calling for help? The next moment he collapsed.

Alice had gone into town on an errand, and she returned to see the ambulance pulling out of the road that leads to their farm. She rode with Martin to the hospital. I remembered Emily Dickinson: "Because I could not stop for Death, he kindly stopped for me." What else could she do but go along for the ride, at least as far as the border? When Chekhov lay dying of tuberculosis, the doctor ordered champagne for him instead of oxygen.

There will be no funeral and no memorial service. I think of Hans Christian Andersen's instructions to the friend who was composing a funeral march for him. "Most of the people who will walk after me will be children, so make the beat keep time with little steps."

Eric and James and I jumped into the car, and drove to the Provensen farm. Friends had been dropping in all day. We sat around the table in the kitchen; the coffeepot was steaming, and everywhere we saw signs of Martin's life on earth. His cap and jacket hung on the hook by the door, his heart medicine stood on the kitchen shelf.

Their daughter, Karen, returned from the funeral parlor.

"I saw Dad," she said. "He was wearing his favorite red-checked shirt. I sat by the coffin and talked and talked. I'm so glad I could say good-bye."

Alice stood up.

"I should go to the funeral parlor too," she exclaimed.

Martin's best friend touched her arm.

"No," he said. "You said good-bye to him in the ambulance. The real Martin isn't in the funeral parlor. You know he always said he didn't believe in the body."

For artists, for writers, what body is there but the body of work we leave behind?

MARCH 30

I can't even imagine what it would be like to lose someone with whom you had done fifty-six books. Going to work every morning for Alice and Martin did not mean the separation that it does for so many couples—he leaves for one office, she for another. Day after day in the studio, the only voices they heard were each other's.

When I saw the obituary for Martin in the *New York Times*, I understood why we need poems. Facts tell us everything and nothing. I happened to mention this paradox to a gentleman who runs one of the two bookshops in our neighborhood, and he told me a story his Irish grandfather told him, a story which may be another way of saying the same thing. The god Lir created the world by speaking the names of everything in it. Because he had only half a tongue, his words were only half understood. Half of creation, therefore, remained unspoken. That's why we need poets: to sing the hidden side of things.

APRIL 3

I've set my story aside to write an elegy for Martin. Chekhov, as always, has good advice: "When you . . . wish to move your readers to pity, try to be colder. It will give a kind of backdrop to . . . grief, make it stand out more. . . . Yes, be cold" (Troyat, p. 148).

APRIL 6

Worked on the elegy. Literature from Bread Loaf is arriving. Oh, Chekhov would have enjoyed that place. He might have been talking about Bread Loaf and not the Crimea when he confessed to family and friends, "I haven't written a line . . .", "I'm gradually turning into a talking machine. Now that we've solved all existing problems, we've started in on problems never raised before. We talk and talk and talk; we may die of inflammation of the tongue and vocal cords" (Troyat, 97).

Chekhov could have run a fine workshop, judging from the critiques he gave to writers who sent him manuscripts. How did he find time to answer them all?

You have so many modifiers that the reader has a hard time determining what deserves his attention, and it tires him out. If I write, "A man sat down on the grass," it is understandable because it is clear. . . . But it would be hard to follow and brain-taxing were I to write, "A tall narrow-chested, red-bearded man of medium height sat down noiselessly, looking around timidly and in fright, on a patch of green grass that had been trampled by pedestrians." The brain can't grasp all that at once, and . . . fiction ought to be immediately . . . graspable. (Troyat, 223)

194

APRIL 11

I finished the elegy for Martin.

APRIL 13

As I trudged to the post office to mail the poem to the *New Yorker*, I remembered my favorite rejection letter, written by the editors of a Chinese journal, which appeared in a London paper:

We have read your manuscript with boundless delight. If we were to publish your paper, it would be impossible for us to publish any work of a lower standard. And as it is unthinkable that in the next thousand years we shall see its equal, we are, to our regret, compelled to return your divine composition, and to beg you a thousand times to overlook our short sight and timidity. (*The Writer's Home Companion*, James Charlton and Lisbeth Mark, New York: Franklin Watts, 1987, p. 28)

APRIL 25

Worked on my story.

MAY 20

A call from Anatole Broyard at the *New York Times*. Would I review a book on Dvorak in America? The review should be eight hundred words.

Chekhov's advice to a young writer who felt pressured for time seems to be meant for me.

Stop trying to meet deadlines. I do not know what your income is: if it is small, then starve, as we starved in our youth, but keep your observations for works you . . . write during the blissful hours of inspiration, not in one go. (Troyat, p. 71)

Broyard described the book he wished to send me: *Spillville*, by Patricia Hampl. A pilgrimage to the small town in Iowa where Dvorak spent a summer. The more he talked, the more interesting it sounded.

I thought of Chekhov. I asked myself—do I have the time? I want to finish my story, and I'm going to be in Ann Arbor again at the end of May, taking care of my mother.

Because he told me I have the whole month of June to write it, I said yes.

MAY 22

The galleys I'm to review arrived, along with a fat book on Dvorak, which Broyard thought would help, and a note telling me the review is due June 3. Did I mishear the date or did he change it? I've started to work on it right away.

MAY 23

"There are two worlds, the post office and nature," wrote Thoreau in his journal (January 3, 1853). "I know them both."

Today I got a letter from a child who asked: Are you famous? Are any of your books a movie yet?

I wrote back and said no to both questions. But who knows what tomorrow's mail will bring? When Random House issued a new edition of *The History of Henry Esmond*, the editors received a letter from a Hollywood agent addressed to William Makepeace Thackeray. "In the event that you have already made a commitment to some agent for the above book, we nevertheless are impressed with your potential possibilities as a screen writer and would be interested in both your services and future stories." What a prime candidate for the dead letter office.

Random House replied as follows: "Thank you for your letter. . . . I am now working on a new novel which I think will be a natural for pictures. I am thinking of calling the new book, *Vanity Fair.*" (*The Writer's Home Companion*, pp. 66–67)

MAY 25

A fit of gardening has thrown my back out of kilter; I can't even climb out of bed. My review is due at the end of the week. Lying on my back, I tried to write, but the ink in my pen has no imagination and refuses to flow uphill. The bed is a stagnant sea of papers, books, and cats.

Oh, I should have taken Chekhov's advice.

MAY 26

"A man may write at any time," said Samuel Johnson, "if he will set himself doggedly to it."

I crept out of bed and found that by kneeling at the PC, I could write a little. Anyone seeing me would have supposed I was praying for inspiration. Well, why not kneel to write? Writers have practiced their craft and sullen art in all sorts of positions. Hemingway wrote standing up. So did Virginia Woolf and Lewis Carroll. Proust and Joyce wrote in bed. Rilke says kneeling is the right spiritual posture for an artist.

He who kneels, who gives himself wholly to kneeling, loses the measure of his surroundings . . . he . . . belongs to that world in which height is— depth—and . . . who could measure the depth? (*Letters of Rainer Maria Rilke*, Vol. II, New York: W. W. Norton Company, Inc., 1948, pp. 238–39)

MAY 28

The review for the *Times* is done. Mailed it off this morning.

JUNE 1

I'm in Ann Arbor taking care of Mother. On the way back from the train station, we stopped to visit the grave of her firstborn son, who died three hours after he was born. Years later, when I was growing up, she still talked about him, calculating his age, wondering what kind of person he'd have become.

"I heard him cry," she'd tell me. "I heard the doctor say he'd fit in a teacup. The nuns told me they'd baptized him."

Now he lies under a small headstone in the infant section of the cemetery, in the flock of stone lambs marking the surrounding graves. That boy I was born to replace. Today Mother looks at the grave without interest.

"I can't remember my wedding," she says suddenly. "Did I have a wedding?"

"You did," I say. "You were married at home. You had a luncheon afterwards."

Silence.

"Was I a good mother? I can't remember."

"You were a wonderful mother," I said. "You still are."

"Wasn't I lucky to have you!" she beams. "Think of all the daughters I could have had. My mother was wonderful too," she adds proudly. Pause. "She was so good at taking away pain."

I think of Emerson at seventy, stricken with what we now know was Alzheimer's, fighting his memory loss by sticking labels onto things, describing their use. The names meant nothing to him any more. The sign on his umbrella read: the thing that strangers take away. So he spent the last years of his life living among riddles he made himself. At Longfellow's funeral he murmured to a friend, "That gentleman had a sweet, beautiful soul, but I have entirely forgotten his name."

Easy enough to riddle an umbrella. Not so easy to riddle a human life. The sphinx asks, and Oedipus answers. What goes on four legs in the morning, two legs at noon, and three in the evening?

Last night, Mother was up till four, checking the doors and asking questions. Always the same questions, but sometimes, when the muse is with me, I hear them differently. I listen the way those Irish poets listened who wanted to speak for the dark side of creation.

I have gone to bed in my old room, which still has the luminous stars that my father pasted on the ceiling so many years ago. My mother stands in the hall, her shadow falling into my room. The whole universe sparkles between us.

"Where are we?" she asks. "Who's with us? Where did we come from? Will we still be here tomorrow?"

Close Encounters of the Story Kind

O N C E upon a time an editor, knowing my fascination with angels, invited me to write a story about one, and I thought, "Here's an assignment after my own heart," and I said yes. Then I panicked.

What did I know about angels?

The first angel I saw had a chipped nose. It was blond, male, and lived in a clock, which hung in the parlor of the apartment Mrs. Lear rented in my grandmother's house in Owosso, Michigan. When the hour struck, two doors opened at the top, and a tiny platform revolved, bearing the archangel Michael from one door to the next. Such dignity, such beauty—he was a procession of one. Mrs. Lear's husband had fought in the first world war and brought it from Germany, along with a Luger and some empty shells. A local jeweler who repaired it told him that it must have once held other figures, probably Adam and Eve being driven from the garden. Time had taken the archangel's sword, the fugitives, and the tip of his holy nose. Nevertheless, when I knew the hour was preparing to strike, I would knock on Mrs. Lear's door and ask to see the angel, moving from darkness into darkness. When the novelty wore off and I no longer asked, Mrs. Lear would knock on my grandmother's apartment to announce the angel was marching and did I want to watch it?

An angel marching from darkness into darkness—such an event should not go unnoticed.

The second angel I saw was a picture from an old insurance calendar that my grandmother had saved long after the year was out. A young woman in a white nightgown is standing with arms outstretched over two children playing at the edge of a cliff. There is a large asterisk of apple butter on her wings, as if someone had hurled a full jar during an argument and the angel had taken a blow intended for someone else. The calendar hung in my grandfather's treatment room, where patients with rheumatism and asthma came to avail themselves of the wonders of osteopathy. Only the angel and our family knew that the treatment room had once been a pantry and the waiting room doubled as the doctor's bedroom; my grandfather unfolded the sofa at night to sleep and in the morning folded it up again before the office opened. Grandmother, who managed the renting of the other rooms, had her own quarters off the kitchen.

Though I have seen many pictures of angels since these two, they seem the real ones, the standard by which all others should be measured.

Two days after I'd agreed to write a book about angels, my sister Kirsten called from Ann Arbor with bad news.

"Mother fell and broke her hip," she said, "so I grabbed the first plane out of Pittsburgh last night. The doctor said he wants to give her a new one."

"A new hip? At eighty-seven?"

"He said it's her only chance of walking. And it's manmade, so it's even better than her old one. It will last forever."

"Is she conscious?"

"She's right here. I'll put her on the phone."

I pressed my ear to the receiver and heard nothing.

"Mother? How are you feeling?"

She did not answer for a long time, and when she did, she sounded far off, as if she were speaking from a different room.

"Isn't it the limit I should have to go through this?" she whispered.

A long silence, broken by Kirsten's voice.

"I found Mother's purse. It's been missing for two months. And now we can't find her teeth. They've simply vanished for good and all."

"How long will she be in the hospital?"

"A week. They like to get you out early here. But we'll need round-the-clock care when she moves home."

"What about bringing her to Shady Park?" I asked. "Can they keep her?"

From the house she'd lived in for fifty years my mother moved to a single large room in Shady Park Manor, a convalescent home in Pittsburgh five blocks from my sister and her husband. She had a room of her own. Kirsten made sure of that. On its bare surfaces my sister put spindles of snapshots; on its white walls she hung the brass filigree frames that kept us all in line: me in my cap and gown standing beside Daddy in the cap and gown he only wore when pressed into marching at commencement; my sister in her wedding dress, rising from a swirl of lace; the grandchildren, who had long ago outgrown their school portraits; Mother's diploma from Michigan, its blue and gold ribbon faded but intact. The bureau held her lavender underwear, her nylons, her purple shoes. The closet held all ten of her best purple dresses.

This was the room I saw when I arrived from New York. My classes at Vassar were finished; Kirsten and John would be gone for two weeks. The note in the kitchen laid out my duties.

"Please take in the mail, water the plants in the dining room, and feed the tortoise. He only eats scraped carrots. Scraper is on sink. Please take Mother's dresses to the laundromat and wash them on DELICATE. They wash everything in hot water at the home."

Every morning I walked the five blocks to Shady Park, past the Fourth Presbyterian Church and the synagogue, past the Greek restaurant, the Cafe del Sol, the Korean grocer who hangs strings of jade beads in the window among the melons. Past Eat'n Park, where families carry heaping plates from the salad bar and single men sit at the counter, drinking coffee and smoking. Past Jacov's Vegetarian Deli and Tucker's Secondhand Books.

Shady Park Manor stands over all, at the top of a steep hill. I hurry through the lobby, beautifully decorated in silver and blue wallpaper, up the stairs past the nurse's station. When I arrive at my mother's room she is sitting up in her chair, asleep, belted in, like a passenger in a plane about to land—but somewhere deep in the body of the plane, the fatigued metal has given way and sent this one woman, still strapped to her seat, hurtling through space.

Over my mother's bed, someone has taped a list of instructions.

7:30: Get Mrs W. up to eat breakfast. Be sure dentures are in with fast-teeth powder.
8:00–2:00: Keep Mrs W. up once she is in chair. She will fight to go back to bed, but she needs to be kept active.

"Mom," I say, "wake up!"
She opens her eyes.
"What is this place?"

"A condominium," I lie. "Come on, Ma, let's get the wheelchair and go for a spin around the block."

"Why can't I walk? What's the matter with me?"

"You broke your hip."

I unfold the wheelchair and lift her into it. She is staring at my feet.

"You need new shoes," she says.

We both gaze down at my scuffed loafers. Miles of pavement have pared the heels away and loosened the stitching.

"Promise me you'll buy a new pair. Take some money from my purse. Where is my purse?"

I hand it to her. She opens it and peers in and twitches up a five-dollar bill.

"Didn't I have more money than this when I started?"

"Oh, Mother, you don't need any money here."

"Is this an old people's home?"

"It's a condominium, Ma."

"It's a home. I never thought my children would put me in a home."

"Ma, you need twenty-four-hour care."

"What did people do in the old days?"

What *did* they do? Dutiful daughters struggled with lifting, feeding, and changing their aged parents. I thought of my mother under the stress of caring for her own mother, who lived with us when I was growing up. Does my mother remember the night she got up to go to the bathroom and passed out from exhaustion? She landed against the radiator. Now, at the edge of her short sleeve I can see the long scar on my mother's arm, deep as a knife wound, where the flesh burned slowly away as she lay, numb to the pain. These dutiful women—caregivers is the current term for them—did not go off to jobs in the morning. And they certainly were not writers.

We pass the nurse's station and the board that lists the day's activities. Talking Book Club, Pet Therapy, Monday Night Movie, Bingo, Current Events, Sensory Stimulation, this month's birthdays. In the all-purpose room, the physical therapist is tossing a beach ball to a group of men and women in wheelchairs. None of them raise their arms. As I wheel Mother outside into the sunshine, she raises a pleading face to mine.

"Can't you find a little corner in your house for me?"

In the evening, when I unlock the door of my sister's house, the tortoise creeps out of his shell and crosses the kitchen floor to meet me. His ancient eyes blink when I scrape his carrots, letting the shavings pile up on the plate like golden pages. Outside in the shimmering heat, children play hide and seek and call to each other. The bedroom is suffocating. I carry my sheet and pillow downstairs and make a bed on the living room floor. I read another chapter in John Gardner's *The Art of Fiction* and underline a sentence that sounds like good advice, if only I knew how to follow it: "Fiction does its work by creating a dream in the reader's mind." The last sound I hear before falling asleep is the tortoise taking his constitutional, the faint scraping of his claws along the floor.

Have I told you everything? No. I have not told you how every evening I sat down at my brother-in-law's electric portable and worked on my story. A story about an angel.

The hardest part of writing a story or a novel is beginning it. A letter that arrived recently from a friend of mine whose first novel got rave reviews opens with these words: "So painful coming into possession of a new novel. There is a deep agenda, and I sometimes think I haven't the faintest clue what it is. Still, every day, here I am, at my table, facing it and struggling with lethargy." The material of a story offers itself to the writer like a house in which all the doors and windows are locked. Whose story is it? Whose voice does it belong to? The opening sentence is the key, the way into the house. It may let you in at the front door like a homeowner or at the window like a thief, but it lets you in.

For my angel story, I had no opening sentence. But I had a great many notes on angels, particularly those I deemed useful to writers. Uriel the angel of poetry and Raphael the angel of healing led the list. And how many angels there are, for every problem and purpose! There is an angel who presides over memory and an angel who presides over time, even an angel who presides over Monday. There is an angel for small birds and an angel for tame beasts, an angel for solitude and an angel for patience and an angel for hope. The angel who watches over footstools can offer you a pillar of light to support you, a gift that Hemingway and Virginia Woolf would have appreciated since both wrote standing up.

I also noted the angels who presided over conditions that writers pray to be spared. Barakiel is the angel of chance; Michael, the angel of chaos and insomnia; Harbonah, the angel of annihilation; and Abaddon, the angel of the abyss.

But among the angels, who can really tell which are for us and which against us? There is an angel who presides over hidden things. Forgotten names, lost notes, misplaced drafts—does he hide them or find them? There is an angel of odd events. Are they gifts or griefs, lucky accidents or lost opportunities?

Notice, I didn't say I wrote my story. I said, *worked on it*. What did I really know about angels? How do we come to know things as a writer? I looked at my notes, but no story came. What was I looking for? I made tea. I thought of how other writers prepared to face the blank page. Balzac drank fifty cups of coffee a day, till it killed him; Disraeli put on evening clothes; George Cohan rented a Pullman car drawing room and traveled till he was done with the book or story. Emerson took walks. Colette's husband locked her in her room, and Victor Hugo gave his clothes to his servant with instructions to return them when he was done.

After struggling with the story for three days, I understood the problem. This story had the shape of the one I'd just finished writing. What we've just written lays its shadow on the next work, and it can happen with any length, any genre. A friend who was working on her second novel told me, "It took me two years to break the spell of my first book when I started my second. I kept wanting to repeat what had worked so well. Combinations of characters, scenes." Writing is like panning for gold. You put your pan down close to the mother lode and scoop up a handful of gravel. You know the grains of ore are sparkling in front of you, if only you could see them. Knowing this, even when you find nothing but broken stones, it's hard to throw them away.

So I wrote a story about angels. I wrote badly. I was on the wrong track, but I didn't have the courage to throw those pages away, for then I'd have nothing. Keats was right. All writing is a form of prayer. Was anybody out there listening?

Let me say right now that I don't think anyone can command the angel to come, though I've known at least one person to try, a nun who told her first graders about the guardian angels they'd received at baptism and then said, "I want you all to move over and make room for your angel." Twenty-five first graders shifted to the right and made room for the incorporeal and the invisible. *That* is perfect faith. The nephew who told me the story takes a more skeptical view of angels now.

None of this would be worth telling if I hadn't promised my sister that I'd wash Mother's clothes at the laundromat, and what shouldn't happen did happen. I had a simple plan. I would sit with Mother till noon. While she ate her lunch in the dining room, I would carry the laundry basket over to the Wash Bored and read *The Art of Fiction* and work on my story while the clothes were spinning. And maybe I could take lunch down the street at Jacov's Vegetarian Deli. It had been closed all week, but a sign promised it would be open on Monday.

I arrived at Shady Park around eleven and headed for Mother's room. A thin, white-haired woman was walking toward me on crutches, leaning heavily on stout Miss Davidson, the physical therapist. Miss Davidson beckoned me over.

"I've been trying to get your mom to walk. She doesn't try. She won't even stand up for me. See if you can get her to make an effort."

"I'll do my best," I said.

"Now Beulah here is doing fine," said Miss Davidson.

The woman on crutches nodded.

"I walk every chance I get," she said. "Miss Davidson says, 'Well, how about heading back to your room now?' and I say, 'It hurts, but let's go just once more, up and down the corridor.' I can't wait to go home."

Miss Davidson frowned at me.

"Medicare won't pay for your mother's room if she's not taking part in the physical therapy program."

"Is she doing any activities?" I asked hopefully.

"She likes the crafts," said Miss Davidson. "She made a purple flyswatter out of felt yesterday. And she had the kitten on her lap the whole day."

"What kitten?" I asked.

"Pet therapy," said Beulah. "Your mother wouldn't let anyone else have it. Kept it on her lap the whole time."

When I walked into her room, Mother was asleep in her chair.

"Ma," I said, "I hear you had a kitten."

She opened her eyes.

"What kitten?" she said.

"She forgot already," said Beulah, leaning in the doorway. Mother turned to her.

"My husband taught for forty-seven years at the University of Michigan. We have a total of twenty-two degrees in our family, all from Michigan."

"Isn't that nice," said Beulah. "Now me, I never went to college. My papa worked in the steel mill, and so did my husband till it shut down. I'm going downstairs in the wheelchair. They have Kool-Aid on the terrace."

We heard her thumping back to her room. Mother gave me an odd look.

"Why are you carrying a box of soap?" she asked.

"I'm going to wash your clothes."

And I heaved the laundry basket onto one hip. Lavender plastic; my sister had picked it especially for her.

"You're a good girl," she said and smiled. "Lord, I'm just an ordinary mother. How did I get two such wonderful daughters?"

I wheeled her downstairs, and we sat on the terrace with Beulah till lunchtime. The only other patient was a thin, silent man in a wheelchair and a young woman who sat beside him asking,

"Grandpa, can you talk? Can you talk, Grandpa?"

"That's Mr. Levine," said Beulah. "He's a hundred and two. The president sent him a telegram." She leaned forward and whispered in my ear, "You ask him how old he is and he shouts, 'A hundred and two.' There's not much else he knows. He has Alzheimer's. And he still has a full head of hair."

"What disease do I have?" asked Mother.

"You broke your hip," I said.

"I've had lots of broken bones," said Beulah. "Last year I broke my arm."

Mother stared down at her own arm, the scarred one, as if it had just been brought for her approval.

"How old it looks," she said softly.

The Laundry Bored was nearly empty. A woman was sitting under the lone hairdryer, reading a magazine from which the cover had been ripped away. I threw Mother's clothes in the machine, dialed it to WARM, and poured in the soap. I put *The Art of Fiction* and my box of Tide in the laundry basket and strolled half a block to Jacov's Vegetarian Deli.

The restaurant was tiny—no more than five tables. A sign on the wall read "Tel Aviv, Jerusalem, Ben Gurion Airport. Discover your Roots!" Only one other customer, an elderly man in a black suit, was waiting at the take-out counter for his order. The two cooks wore yarmulkes, yet how different the same garment looked on each of them. The older man was clean-shaven and middle-aged. When he chopped the onions, he seemed to be murdering them. He poured coffee as if it were poison, he shoved a plate of dumplings at the elderly man like a punishment. The younger cook had a thick blond beard and kindly blue eyes, and he loped from the stove to the ice box to the counter as if he had not a care in the world.

The menu over the counter listed vegetable soup and vegetarian pizza.

"I'll have soup," I said. "What kind of dumplings did you just give that man?"

"You won't like them," said the sour cook.

"I'll have them anyway," I said.

"Try one first," said the young cook, "and if you like it, I'll give you a plateful."

He handed me a dumpling on a paper plate. It tasted like nothing I'd ever eaten before or would want to eat again. I ordered a plate of them, to spite the sour cook. The elderly gentleman took his paper plate, paused at a small rack on the wall from which he plucked a greasy page. Out of curiosity, I took one also and found it was a page from the Jewish prayer book, Hebrew on one side, English on the other. There was also a pamphlet, *Thought for the Week*, so I took that as well and read it as I munched my dumplings:

> A Thought for the Week:
> Love your fellow Jew as you love yourself.

Alas, I was not a Jew. They would feed me here but they would not love me. I read on:

> Sidra Vayeishev. It is different at home (Part II). Last week we learned that our forefather Jacob did not feel "at home" in the world of material possessions. Knowing that he was only a temporary resident in this physical world he felt that his true "home" was in matters of the Neshama, in Torah and Mitzvos. The world with all its comforts, its palaces and mansions, is nothing more than a tent, erected during the journey of life to sleep over for a night, or rest for a day or two. And on a journey, after all, only the bare

necessities of eating and sleeping are required; but when the journey is over and one comes home . . . well, at home it's different.

When I'd finished the last greasy bite, I put the pamphlet and the prayer sheet in the rack and returned to the laundromat. The lights on the machine were off. The clothes were clean. So was the top of the machine.

The clothesbasket, along with *The Art of Fiction* and my manuscript, had vanished.

Though the day was hot, I felt as cold as if I wore the wind for a cloak. A terrible calm washed over me, leaving me lightheaded. Loss had numbed my capacity to rage.

Suddenly, among the *Reader's Digest*s on the folding table, I spied *The Art of Fiction*. I snatched it up. With shaking fingers I riffled through all the other magazines, shook them, and waited for my manuscript to come out of hiding, like a mischievous child.

Nothing. On this occasion the angel who presides over hidden things was not on my side.

What else was there to do but walk across the street and sit on the bench at the bus stop and consider my life? When the elderly gentleman from Jacov's Deli sat next to me, I was scarcely aware of him till he began to edge closer.

"I notice the subject of your book," he said. "It is a subject dear to my heart. Are you a writer?"

"Yes," I said.

"Stories? You write stories?"

"Stories, a novel, poems," I said.

"I too wrote stories once," he said, "though I am not a writer now. I am a teacher. A teacher of American literature. But I have written stories."

My heart sank. He saw in me a kindred soul. Soon he would press his manuscript upon me. Yet he had used the past tense; perhaps he wrote stories no more. Had his inspiration run dry? Had he lost his memory?

"What kind of stories do you write," he asked, "if I may ask?"

"Short stories," I said.

"Forgive me," he said. "It's like asking the birds what kind of eggs they lay. Blue? Speckled? Large? Small?"

"Look," I said, "I can't really talk about my stories just now.

Somebody just stole the only copy of the story I've been working on for weeks."

"You are sure somebody stole it?" he asked, as if such things did not happen in this world.

"I left it in the laundromat while I was eating lunch. And when I came back—"

"Excuse me," he interrupted, "but may I tell you a story? Long ago there lived in a north province in China a man good at interpreting events. This man had a son, and one day the son's best mare ran away and was taken by the nomads across the border. The son was distraught, but his father said, 'What makes you think this isn't a blessing?' Many months later, the horse returned, bringing with her a magnificent stallion. The son was delighted and mounted the horse, but had scarcely set out for a ride when he fell and broke his hip. Again he was distraught, and again his father said, 'What makes you think this isn't a blessing?' Two years later the nomads invaded and every ablebodied man marched to battle. All were lost. Only the lame son and the elderly father survived. What is blessing and what is disaster?"

"Somebody stole my story. That's a disaster," I said.

Two young women joined us on the bench till one murmured to the other, "I can't stand this heat. I'm going to the drugstore."

"What you need in the drugstore?" said the other.

"Nothing. It's air-conditioned," said the first. "We can look at magazines."

I was about to follow them when the elderly gentleman said,

"Steinbeck's dog chewed the first half of the draft of *Of Mice and Men*. And Steinbeck forgave him, saying, 'I'm not sure Toby didn't know what he was doing when he ate that first draft. I have promoted Toby-dog to be lieutenant-colonel in charge of literature.' You know, I used to write stories. And I almost wrote a novel. I had three hundred pages written in a big notebook. And then the war came. During the war I lost everything."

"How terrible to lose a novel!" I cried. I meant to say, how terrible to lose everything.

He shook his head.

"Really, in my case, it was a blessing. I wanted to write a family history, a bildungsroman. Thomas Mann was my hero. I had notes, a family tree, plans, hundreds of plans. But in my heart of hearts I knew my novel sounded wooden. A wise man said, 'A writer with a fixed idea is like a goose trying to hatch a stone.' In 1940, I was sent to Ravensbrück. All my life my teachers told me not to daydream. Now it was my salvation. Can you outline a dream? Would it be worth dreaming if you could? In that terrible place I let my mind wander, and my characters came back to me, not as I saw them in my notes and plans but as they saw themselves, full of memories and longings. I understood their real story at last. I turned no one away. Does the sea refuse a single river? Have you heard of Van Der Post and his explorations of Africa?"

"No," I said. "Sorry."

"Never mind. He tells of the time he traveled to a village where a great hunter lived. When he arrived, he found the hunter sitting motionless. And the villagers said, 'Don't interrupt him. He is doing work of the utmost importance. He is making clouds.' "

"Did you finish your novel?" I asked. I have a weakness for happy endings.

"How could I finish it? We had no paper. No pens. But we had tongues. So I became a storyteller instead of a writer. I no longer thought of plots, only of voice. Of whose story I was telling. When I hear the voice, I know the story will find me. Storytellers do not lose their stories, except when they die. I like to start my stories in the old style, *once upon a time*. "Once upon a time" is a promise, a promise of a story, and I try to keep my promises. Of course, not everyone agrees with me about these methods. My son, for example. He's a TV writer. Weekends, he wants to write the great American novel, but he doesn't know how to get started. One day he calls me from New York, all excited. 'I've just signed a contract to write the bible!' Naturally I'm interested. He goes on to say that this bible is not from God, of course. This is the book TV script writers use when they're doing a new series of shows. It describes characters, it describes place, it describes adventures.

" 'And for what show are you writing a bible?' I ask my son.

" 'It's a mini-series,' he says. 'It's called *The Further Adventures of Alice in Wonderland*.'

" 'How can that be?' I say. 'There is only one Lewis Carroll.'

" 'Yes, Papa, but there are five script writers. They'll make up the other adventures. But they can write only about what they know. I'm going to write them a detailed description of Wonderland and the characters.' What do you think, fellow-scribbler? Is it a good idea, the further adventures of *Alice in Wonderland*?"

"I don't know," I said. "What happened to your son?"

"My son read the Alice books carefully. He mapped the terrain, noted the architecture, the dangers, the geography, the birds and animals. He wrote out character studies of everyone mentioned in the books. And he got paid well. And suddenly a brilliant idea struck him. Why not write a bible for his great unwritten American novel? How much easier it would be to start his novel if he had a detailed knowledge of his characters. Hadn't his English teachers always said, 'Write about what you know'?"

"My teachers said the same thing," I laughed.

"They all say it," said the elderly gentleman. "I even said it to my students. But I didn't mean my students should write such a bible. If you take everyone's advice, you'll build a crazy house. My son wrote out descriptions of all his characters and their locale. Then he wrote the first two chapters and showed them to me. 'Aaron,' I said, 'how can I tell you? This is from your head, not your heart. It's predictable. No surprises. Even God is surprised by the actions of his creatures.'

" 'I've put a lot of time into this,' he said.

" 'The nest is done, but the bird is dead,' I told him. 'You should take a lesson from your Lewis Carroll. He was a storyteller. I know for a fact that when he sent his Alice down the rabbit hole, he didn't know what would happen next. That white rabbit was a gift from Providence. We should follow Providence, not force it.' He's intelligent, my Aaron, but he thinks too much. He needs intelligence to keep him from hindering himself so he is free to do amazing things. I tell him to watch Charlie Chaplin. You have seen his great film *Modern Times*?"

"A long time ago," I said, hoping he wouldn't quiz me on it.

"Maybe you remember, near the end, Charlie has to go on the stage and sing a song. And now he can't remember the words. So Paulette Goddard writes the words on his cuff. He goes onstage, he tries to read them, he's hopeless. Not a sound out of him. He's paralyzed. And then Paulette Goddard calls out, 'Never mind the words. Just sing.' "

"I think that kind of thing happens only when you tell stories," I said, "not when you write them."

"It can also happen when you write them," he said. "You have two choices. You can arrange the material, with outlines. Or you can arrange yourself. I see you looking at the laundromat. You have business there?"

"I forgot to put my mom's clothes in the dryer."

"And you want to see if the thief returned your manuscript." he added.

"Yes," I agreed.

Suddenly I remembered my promise.

"Excuse me," I said, rising. "Do you know a good shoe store?"

"From writing to shoes!" he said and laughed.

"I have to run. I promised my mother I'd buy some new shoes."

"Are you in such a hurry?" he exclaimed. "Let me tell you about a man who set out to buy himself shoes. He measured his foot and put the measurements away. When he got to the market, he found he'd left the measurements at home. He chose a pair of shoes and hurried home for the measurements, but when he returned the market was closed. He never got the shoes, of course. And that night he dreamed his feet asked him, 'Why didn't you trust us? Why did you trust the measurements more than your own feet?' "

We stood up in unison.

"There's a department store one street over," he said. "But all shoe stores are good if you need shoes."

I didn't go shopping for shoes, and I didn't find my manuscript. When I arrived at Shady Park, Mother was not in her room. She had been wheeled into the TV room. She was asleep, her head nearly on her chest; she had been left at a long empty table with her back to the TV. Probably she had told the attendant that she didn't like television. The other chairs were all facing the set, as if their occupants were worshipping it.

I rushed in and turned her chair around.

"Wake up, Ma. We're going back to your room."

But Mr. Levine's chair was stuck in the doorway, blocking it. He was making helpless swoops with his hands, trying to move the wheels.

"Let me help you," I said, and pushed him through.

Instantly a ripple of movement started behind me, as if I had waked the very walls.

"Lady, can you help me?"

"Miss, can you get me out of here? Miss!"

Heads lifted, hands waved.

"Miss!"

I can't help them all, I thought.

"Mother, do you want to look at the box of photographs with me?"

"I want to lie down," she said.

What angel was present in the room with us on that evening? The angel of chance or the angel of memory? The angel of time or the angel of hidden things? After I'd put away her dresses, clean but crumpled from being carried in my arms, I sat on the edge of her bed and flipped through the box of snapshots. Tucked in among the pictures were Christmas cards. Mother never threw away a Christmas card that had a photograph on it. I held up a picture of an elderly couple standing in front of the Taj Mahal.

"Who in thunder are they?" exclaimed Mother.

"I don't know," I said. "Let me read you the writing on the back. 'We visited fourteen countries and had a wonderful time. Love, Dorothy and Jack.' "

"Are both my parents dead?" asked Mother.

"Oh, Ma, you know they died a long time ago. If they were alive, they'd be a hundred and twenty."

I pulled out another picture and held it up. It showed a middle-aged woman standing on what appeared to be a cistern and smiling. I turned the photograph over and read the scrawled inscription.

"This is your old Aunt Velda standing by the well. Clark covered it over for me and put in running water, hot and cold. He also made the driveway you can see behind me, to the left."

Mother's face brightened.

"I remember that well," she said. "There was a pump on Grandpa's farm in Iowa. Oh, he had acres and acres of the best farmland in the county. And when the men were working in the fields, Grandma would fill a bucket of water from that pump. And she'd send me out with the bucket and dipper to give the men a drink. And it seemed like such a long walk coming and going, I was dying of thirst by the time I got back to the house. And Grandma wouldn't let me pour myself a drink from the pump right off. No. She made me hold my wrists under the spout, and she'd pump and pump the water over them. To cool my blood, she said, so the cold drink wouldn't give me a stomachache. Lord, how good that cold water felt. And how good it tasted."

I'd never heard her tell this story. How many other stories lay hidden in her heart, waiting for a listener to wake them?

Suddenly I understood my real task. I would lay my angel story aside and forget about it for a while. Tomorrow I would bring a notebook and start writing down her memories. I would have to be patient. Memory has nothing to do with outlines and everything to do with accidents.

On my way home I stopped once more at the Wash Bored and couldn't believe my eyes. There on top of the fateful washing machine stood the clothes basket. And safe in its plastic lavender embrace nestled my story.

I pulled it out and turned the pages, checking them for bruises. I counted the pages. I pulled up a chair and reread them. Was the angel of hope responsible for what happened next?

I threw the entire manuscript in the wastebasket. I would take Rilke's advice: "If the angel deigns to come, it will be because you have convinced him, not by tears, but by your horrible resolve to be a beginner."

Voices. Voices. That night, before I fell asleep, I heard the voices of my characters, though faintly, like a conversation accidentally picked up on a long-distance line. I did not let them know I was listening.

The next morning I set out for Shady Park Manor with a light heart and was pleasantly surprised to meet my storyteller coming out of the synagogue at the end of the block.

"You are going to visit your mother? May I walk with you as far as Jerry's Good and Used?"

"What's Jerry's Good and Used?"

"Jerry has this and that of everything. His specialty is baseball cards. He calls last night and says, 'I have a treasure. Something you want very much, a card of the great Japanese ballplayer, Sadaharu Oh.' He asks me why I want a card of Sadaharu Oh. I tell him that I want a picture of the man who wrote in his autobiography not about winning but about waiting. Waiting, he says in that book, is the most active state of all. It is the beginning of all action. Did you find your manuscript?"

"I found it. And I threw it away. I'm starting over. This time I'll wait for the story to find me. Like you said yesterday."

I expected my new acquaintance to offer his congratulations, but he did not.

"The freedom of the dream doesn't mean doing nothing. You still have to sit down every day and write. What if the angel came and you were out shopping for shoes? God helps the drowning sailor, but he must row. You have a long journey ahead of you. And it starts with one footstep."

"It feels more like an ending than a beginning," I said.

"Endings and beginnings—are they so far from each other? When I was in Ravensbrück, I was chosen to die. Only because someone among the killers recognized me was I saved. Now when I tell my stories, I remember that moment. It makes the telling more urgent. How is your mother?"

"Fine, I guess. Just very tired."

"You know, when I was little, my mother would put me to sleep by describing rooms in all the houses she'd lived in. And so many things happened in those rooms. Now you can hardly find a house in which someone has died or been born. It all happens away from us, in big hospitals."

"My mother told me a story yesterday," I said. And I described to him my mother's journey to the harvest fields with the bucket of water, and the journey back to the well, and the cold water on her wrists.

He was silent for so long that I felt I had said something foolish.

"The cold water—it's such an unimportant detail," I remarked.

"Unimportant?" he exclaimed. "That is why it's worth remembering. When I was young I fell in love with a girl named Hilda, who happened to be a twin. I asked her to go out with me. She agreed to go, but only if I could tell her apart from her sister. I studied her face for several minutes. Then she ran and got her twin. Hilda had a blue vein on the bridge of her nose. Unimportant, a blue vein, but when I spied it, I knew I was saved."

"I'll save that detail about the cold water for my next story," I assured him.

He wagged a finger at me.

"Don't save it. Use it, use it now. You just threw out your life savings. This is no time for prudence."

We passed Jerry's Good and Used. My storyteller did not go in. Instead he kept pace with me, up the hill to Shady Park Manor.

"May I tell you a story as we take this little walk together? Long ago, when wizards still walked the length and breadth of the earth, there arrived in the world of the dead a great magician.

" 'Why have you come here?' asked the Mistress of the Dead.

"The magician explained that when he was building his boat he found he could not finish it without four magic words, and that he had not been able to find them, however far he traveled.

" 'The Lord of the Dead will never teach you his spells,' answered the Mistress of the Dead.

"But the magician could not give up the task of finishing his boat. He wandered here and there until one day he met a shepherd who told him to seek out the giant.

" 'In his vast mouth there are a hundred magic words. You will have to go down into his enormous belly, and there you will learn marvels. But it's not easy to get there. You must go along a path leaping on the points of women's needles, and over a cross-road paved with sharp swords, and down a third road made of the blades of heroes' axes.'

"But the magician was determined to try it. He would do anything to find those four words and finish his boat. Four words! Marvelous words! Would you believe I once bought a photography book because of a single sentence? I was standing in Tucker's—it's a block down the street from us—and I opened up a book and read the epigraph on the first page. It was the beginning and the ending of *Finnegan's Wake.*

> A way a lone a last a loved
>> along the riverrun,
>>> past Eve and Adam's

Right away I wanted to read *Finnegan's Wake.* But Tucker's didn't have it. And the library was closed for a week. But how could I live without those words? So I bought the photography book. I bought it for those words."

We arrived at Shady Park.

"It is good you are listening to your mother."

"I'm going to write her memories down. I don't want to forget them."

"If you forget a few, don't worry. What you need will come back to you. We don't really understand something until we have forgotten it. Live in your roots, not in your branches."

I took the elevator to the second floor. When I stepped out, a nurse hurried up to me.

"Your mother had a seizure last night. We phoned for the ambulance just an hour ago. Call Dr. Rubin right away—you can use the phone at the nurse's station."

The voice of medical authority at the other end of the phone named the problem: status epilepticus. Dr. Rubin explained he had given her Valium and phenobarbital.

"It took us over an hour to stop her seizures. Now she's asleep."

"Did she have a stroke?"

"This morning I thought yes. When I looked at the CAT scan, I thought no. Her brain is shrunken, and there's an abnormal pattern of electric ions. It's probably caused by the little strokes she's had earlier."

"I'll be right over."

I hung up, and the nurse touched my arm.

"I'm so sorry," she said. "Let me call you a cab."

I waited downstairs for the cab. The receptionist was changing the bulletin board, posting the new activities. Bingo, Sensory Stimulation, Current Events, Patio Outing.

A way a lone a last a loved along the riverrun.

Dr. Rubin and I are standing by my mother's bed in the intensive care section. Mother is sleeping under the watchful gaze of the IV and the blood pressure basket hanging over her bed, its black tubes coiled into a nest. Over the basket a large plastic bottle bubbles and quakes. This is not the first time I have seen Mother in intensive care.

"When do you think she'll wake up?" I ask.

The doctor shrugs.

"Who knows? It could be tomorrow. It could be in ten minutes. Or it could be never."

I reach out and touch her hair, still soft and wavy, and the translucent skin on her temple: pale freckled silk. The doctor pulls away the plastic respirator that covers the center of her face with a clear green beak, and her sunken cheeks flutter in and out like the throat of a frightened bird. A tube snakes out of her nose, ready for her next feeding. Her mouth is a small black hole. The doctor leans close to her face, as if he might kiss her. Then he pries open her eyelids and looks deeply into her pupils and calls,

"Mrs. Williams! Mrs. Williams!"

Two green-gray coins stare back at him, as cold and indifferent as the eyes of a fish. I feel my knees growing weak, and I sit down fast on the edge of her bed.

"Can she hear us now?"

"Possibly. There's no way of knowing for sure."

When he leaves us alone together, I take her hand, frail as the claw of a wren. The IV has left a deep bruise on her arm. How old it looks, this arm, limp when I lift it, a mottled mineral brown across which white scars move like the shapes of ancient beasts.

I know I will never see her alive again. I do not know if she can hear. I put my mouth close to her ear and tell her I love her. I thank her for telling me about the cold water. I tell that I lost my story in Pittsburgh, a story about angels. I lost it at the laundromat, and I met a man who told me how to find it again. Maybe he wasn't a man at all, maybe he was the story angel? He did not have wings, but who needs wings in Pittsburgh? Though my mouth is touching her ear, I feel my mother going farther and farther away. I want to talk to her till she is out of earshot. Though she is traveling with empty hands, I do not want my mother, who has given me so much, to leave with an empty heart. I give her an angel, a daughter, and herself. And I give her my promise to save them: *once upon a time.*

Acknowledgments

"The Hucklebone of a Saint," "Theo's Girl," and "Sinner, Don't You Waste that Sunday," are taken from *Childhood of the Magician* (Liveright); "Doctrine of the Leather-Stocking Jesus" and "The Well-Tempered Falsehood: The Art of Storytelling," from *Angel in the Parlor* (Copyright © 1982 by Nancy Willard, reprinted by permission of Harcourt Brace Jovanovich, Inc.); "Salvage for Victory," from chapter 28 of *Things Invisible to See* (Alfred A. Knopf); "How Poetry Came into the World and Why God Doesn't Write It," from *The Bread Loaf Anthology of Contemporary American Short Stories* (University Press of New England); "Telling Time," from *The Bread Loaf Anthology of Contemporary American Essays* (University Press of New England).

"Close Encounters of the Story Kind" appeared in *New England Review*.

"Questions My Son Asked Me, Answers I Never Gave Him," "How to Stuff a Pepper," "Moss," "How the Hen Sold Her Eggs to the Stingy Priest," "A Humane Society," "In Praise of ABC," "For You, Who Didn't Know," "Angels in Winter," "When There Were Trees," from *Household Tales of Moon and Water* (Harcourt Brace Jovanovich [the "Material"] [Seq. Num. 25308]); from *Carpenter of the Sun* (Liveright): "Carpenter of the Sun"; from *Water Walker* (Alfred A. Knopf): "A Wreath to the Fish," "Walking Poem," "In Praise of Unwashed Feet," "Onionlight," "The Potato Picker," "Roots," "Marriag Amulet," "Little Elegy with Books and Beasts," "Buffalo Climbs Out of Cellar," "Saints Lose Back," "Divine Child Rolls On."

"The Poet Invites the Moon for Supper," "The Poet Takes a Photograph of His Heart," "The Poet Turns His Enemy into a Pair of Wings," "The Poet's Wife Watches Him Enter the Eye of the Snow," from *19 Masks for the Naked Poet,* copyright © 1971 by Nancy Willard, reprinted by permission of Harcourt Brace Jovanovich, Inc.

"William Blake's Inn for Innocent and Experienced Travelers," "Blake Leads a Walk on the Milky Way," "The King of Cats Sends a Postcard to His Wife," "The Tiger Asks Blake for a Bedtime Story," "Epilogue," from *A*

UNIVERSITY PRESS OF NEW ENGLAND publishes books under its own imprint and is the publisher for Brandeis University Press, Brown University Press, Clark University Press, University of Connecticut, Dartmouth College, Middlebury College Press, University of New Hampshire, University of Rhode Island, Tufts University, University of Vermont, and Wesleyan University Press.

Library of Congress Cataloging-in-Publication Data

Willard, Nancy.
  [Selections. 1991]
  A Nancy Willard reader : selected poetry and prose / Nancy Willard.
      p.   cm. — (The Bread Loaf series of contemporary writers)
  ISBN 0-87451-568-8
  I. Title.   II. Series.
  PS3573.I444A6   1991   91-50377
  818'.5409—dc20   ⊗   CIP